BREAKTHROUGH
MIRACULOUS STORIES OF HEALING AND HOPE

ANITA ANDREAS

ISBN: 978-0615995168

DEDICATION

To the One
who transformed the lives
of my patients
who is worthy of all
honor and glory

To the patients
who leaned into their Beloved
and received the touch
from His kind hand

May you always remember

Praise for
BREAKTHROUGH

More remarkable than the stories that fill these pages, is the woman behind the stories. She is kind, walks in integrity, and continues to reach out to the weak and the hurting. I am thankful to call her friend. She is a gift to the field of occupational therapy.
Daisy Nicholson Burgan, BA, COTA/L
Academic Fieldwork Coordinator/Instructor

BREAKTHROUGH into greater healing for your patients! Anita's testimonies extend an invitation to the medical community to partner with the Holy Spirit as we practice medicine. This book has inspired me to walk into treatment sessions knowing that the Creator and Healer is walking along side of me.
Erin Colvis, MPT

Anita's life is a testimonial of God supernaturally working through a vessel totally yielded to Him. The stories she shares will inspire you to allow God to do the same through you. Look at what God did through the prophet Elijah, and yet the Bible says that he was one "with a nature like OURS" (James 5:16-18) Don't hold back, Go for it. Go for it! Be who you were created to be, and let the testimony of Christ shine through you.
Dan Zacharias, Meteorologist

This book is a blessing to the occupational therapy community and the medical field at large. Anita's experiences and outcomes with her patients are a lovely legacy for the occupational therapy profession. It is a labor of love!
Rachel M. Eisfelder, MOT, OTR/L

The stories in this book are amazing. The pictures she paints of God's touch of healing for her patients are profound and vivid. I felt I could reach out and touch her people; I was right there with her every step of the way.
Penny Frisbie, Social Worker/Intercessor

I have personally seen Anita minister in the Lord as described in her writing. Read and enjoy BREAKTHROUGH and see your faith grow!
Jodie Feldman, Director of Inner City Light/Author/Speaker
www.ICLGlobal.net

CONTENTS

ACKNOWLEDGEMENTS

1 INTRODUCTION 1

2 PARTNERING PRAYER FOR AUTISM Pg 3

3 HOPE FOR BRAIN INJURY Pg 17

4 PROVIDENCE FOR PARKINSONS Pg 28

5 TWO TO TANGO Pg 42

6 FORLORN TO FREEDOM Pg 49

7 LIGHT INVADES THE DARKNESS Pg 58

8 LOVE CONFOUNDS CANCER Pg 69

9 FLOURISHING IN INFANCY Pg 77

10 FROM DEATH'S DOOR Pg 86

11 A SMILE IN THE SPIRIT Pg 94

12 FROM STROKE TO SUCCESS Pg 104

13 RESCUED FROM RESTRICTIONS Pg 114

14 AWAKENING FROM ALZHEIMERS Pg 120

15 COCAINE CHAOS TO TRANQUILITY Pg 135

16 BACKBONE OF A MARRIAGE Pg 146

17 WALKING IN JOY AND PEACE Pg 156

CONCLUSION Pg 170

ACKNOWLEDGEMENTS

There have been dozens who have graciously supported me throughout the writing, editing and publication of this book. I will try to highlight only some here, but am forever grateful to so many others along the way.

I first want to honor my family for all their encouraging words, prayers & cheering me on over the years. Love and gratitude to Josh & Sharon, Shakti, Daniel, Joe & Rachelle, Gry & the grandkids whose lives and hugs inspired me. To my sister & brother, Jackie & Gary & families; your love blessed me.

My heart wells up with gratitude for my 'right-hand woman,' publisher, advisor, & graphic designer Mindy Pamer; she was a constant loyal force pressing me onward. Thanks also to my amazing final proofreaders, who saw this project to completion, Armi Blunda & Andrew Jamieson. What a team!

My Inkwell Writers Group will be forever woven into the fabric of this work with their painstaking attention to detail and yet overwhelming support. Deep thanks to Simmie, Liz, Mary, Dana, Sarah, Colleen, and Cheryl.

Three incredible editors lovingly shared their time and expertise to correct, redirect and teach me editing strategies to transform rather boring reports into real stories about real people. How do I thank you for your patience and gentle nudging to look higher and see possibilities? I will forever recall hours of delving deep with Donna Thomas, Jackie Macgirvin and Sharon Spicca.

Also over the life of this emerging work were numerous faithful intercessors, dear confidants and friends who took time to hear my heart and give a word of love & direction at the right moment. Unending gratitude to Josie, Bonnie, Billie, Jodie, Elaine, Rick & Judy, Linda & Jim, Teri, Stacy, Victoria, Marcia, Peggy, Elaine, Kathie & Tim, Sharon, Jan, Jean, Alan, Jonathan & Erin, Tina, Mary Ann, John, Rose Mary, Kathy, Lisa, Thetis, Dale, Karen, Glenn & Jeff.

I extend deep appreciation and heartfelt thanks to dear friends, professional contributors & colleagues Daisy & Jake, Rachel, Lauren and Erin without whom I couldn't have brought this work to completion.

Sincere appreciation to Rich Harris - Living Word Ministries, pastor & friend, who believed in me, spoke life into me about my writing & who published my first prophetic poem. It set me on a path. Also Stephanie Shureman of The Dwelling Place, thank you for being a constant exhorter into my life.

Deep thanks to my faithful House Church friends, Dave, Ruth, Beth, Ray, Penny, David, Denise, Liz and Dan and our wonderful youth who stood ground with me for this work to glorify the Lord.

ANITA ANDREAS

1

INTRODUCTION

In my thirty years of private medical practice as an occupational therapist, I watched God touch and heal the bodies, minds and spirits of many children and adults. God's pure heart of love for me and my patients became strikingly clear as I witnessed these profound transformations. Led on this journey of faith, it was apparent to me, I was experiencing a God who has great mercy and kindness for His beloved creation. Privileged to see His outstretched arm of love and compassion, I watched the healing of autism, cancer, brain damage, Alzheimer's disease, severe visual deficits, Parkinson's disease, chronic back pain and Attention Deficit Disorder, to name a few.

These are true stories. Though names and places have been changed to maintain confidentiality, I have tried to bring you an authentic record of some of these miraculous events. These astounding healings were seen and confirmed by physical therapists, speech therapists, nurses and doctors working with the patients. The stories are offered to glorify God's Holy Name and bring honor to our Father in heaven who has sovereign authority in every realm. The following events were recorded to build your faith and assure you that Yeshua HaMashiach, Jesus Christ of Nazareth lives today. Through the power of His Holy Spirit, He continues to bring comfort and healing to the sick and broken-hearted through His compassionate heart.

Each story includes valuable reflections with scriptures that give insight and direction related to God's heart and ways. Whether you are a friend or family member of one suffering or a medical caregiver praying for patients, you will find keys for breakthrough in this book. If you are a person challenged with an infirmity or simply someone wanting to understand more about God's healing for today, reading this book will build deeper trust and intimacy with God.

May these stories lift your spirit and reveal the King of kings whose hope and kindness is without end. May the God of goodness and mercy be glorified and honored as you allow these breakthrough stories to touch your hearts. He loves you with an everlasting love and desires to draw you to Himself.

2

PARTNERING PRAYER FOR AUTISUM

I gazed through the natural portal of the crisscrossing eaves as I trudged up the wobbly project stairs to meet my newly assigned home health family. Looking down as I walked, I tried to dodge any stray debris or weak boards. I detected a distant moan of some single mom. *Was that from my destinations doorway?* I hoped not. Rising dread gripped my heart. Entering this zone of despair, hopelessness draped the atmosphere.

Who adored these brave mothers, these young princesses at night, I pondered? *Who exhorted them as they cooled their children's feverish brows with damp cloths at 2AM? Who reassured them with words every worried mother needs to hear? 'It will be all right. By morning he'll be better?'* I thought. Long since, most fathers had fled to find more fertile soil to lay new seed. They had left wives or girlfriends, now made moms to water these tender shoots, the lives of their sweet babies; it was a sea of young mothers doing hard labor, themselves needing nurturing and safe keeping.

A growing mystique arose as I anticipated knocking on Apt 420 to meet Victor and Sarah. I took one last glance at the patches of dirt, checker boarded with areas of dried grass in the project square. Encircled by towering dilapidated structures, identical doorways spanned blocks, each called home by someone. My eyes darted across the panoramic. I yearned to see just one single child bound across the rough turf shouting with joy. Heaving a sigh, I knocked. The peeling dingy door squeaked open only a crack.

I caught a flash of a toddler. Three-year-old Victor came careening past the door. His mom, Sarah glanced behind her. Slowly turning back to me, she forced a weak smile. She pressed the door open against a backlog of toys and rubble scattered across the living room floor. Curtains drawn, a dark haze hung in the air which enveloped my spirit as I entered. I gingerly stepped through an obstacle course, slipping once on a shiny plastic remnant of a deflated ball.

As we sat together on the couch, Sarah's long fingers nervously raked through her thick black hair. As she told her story, she covered tired downcast eyes, flashing an occasional look of a frightened caged animal.

"I have to work extra shifts to keep up, but I hate leaving him with the neighbors. They say that all he does is cry. He cries a lot with me too, though..."

We heard a sound from the next room. Her eyes wandered past me to the bedroom door. We rose by a shared unspoken agreement to find Victor. There he sat. A wiry framed boy sat huddled in the corner, tugging at his t-shirt, rocking, moaning and crying. He seemed unaware of our presence. I reflected on the doctor's reports and assessments which diagnosed him with Attention Deficit Hyperactivity Disorder and Autism. As I watched him, the label seemed to fit.

Sarah knelt down. I sat on the floor near them.

"Victor, come to mama," Sarah coaxed. She reached out to him tenderly. His dark round eyes seemed spellbound in the opposite direction, drawn by an interior world.

"Come here, honey," she cooed. Quite suddenly, however he launched a frenetic leap. By some phenomenal inner prompting, he raced to the far side of the apartment, finding another fortress.

We trailed behind. We found him in a trancelike vigil of poking a nearby toy, randomly rubbing the wall and finally shaking a scrap of paper near his eyes. This sequence all transpired within a one minute time span. His little head tilted, as he focused up and to the left. He appeared to be listening to an inner chorus of chaos and unrest.

Instinctively, I reached out to stroke Sarah's arm. Our hearts seemed to be sharing the heavy burden of Victor's inner torment. We watched together as I prayed silently. I longed to see some sign from Victor of connection to the here and now. Just as I was considering this, he unleashed a scream followed by bitter weeping. He jumped to his feet to seek yet another destination of self-absorption. I looked at Sarah who was struggling to suppress tears. I knew it could be a long road to reach this child. She turned to face me. I sensed dozens of unspoken questions were racing through her mind.

Mustering a confident response, I squeezed her arm in reassurance and said, "He's young and you have reached out for help at an early age. Much can still be done. I'm here now and I'll do everything I can." *Oh Lord, with your help and grace*, I silently prayed.

"Do you know why he won't eat? she erupted.

I retrieved my notepad from the couch. Sarah sat Victor in his highchair. The luncheon tug of war ensued. With bellowing howls and arms flailing, Victor resisted the spoon. The yummy smelling mac 'n cheese went untouched. One of his hands vigorously blocked the approaching utensil while with the other; he shoved chunks of Jell-O into his mouth.

"The only thing he'll eat," she shared, "even though I've tried everything,"

I watched dazed, as Victor deflected every healthier morsel of food from passing his tightly clenched lips. We noted his first therapy goal.

Frazzled, Sarah explained further, "His dad, Harry comes by sometimes, but Victor just runs away. Harry says he thinks Victor doesn't like him, so he doesn't visit much." I jotted another note to remember to talk to Harry. This young dad needed a better understanding of Victor's physiological condition so as not to take it personally. And Sarah needed Harry to understand so she could get more support.

I left that day with much to ponder before I visited Victor at his preschool the following week.

Matronly robust Katherine, an eternally confident and calm veteran teacher spotted me coming through the classroom door. Passing off her juice pitcher to an assistant, she scurried over with a litany of concerns about her darling Victor.

"None of us have seen him make eye contact or smile. What can we do?" she worried. Her impassioned plea was a question I was certain she had asked herself dozens of times. She shared a similar picture of Victor that I saw in his home.

I sighed and nodded as Katherine poured out her heart to me. Apparently, this one child single-handedly had turned their cooperative preschool environment into a constant series of upheavals. Now the staff was looking for fresh insight. They had exhausted every strategy which in the past had proven effective for many children. To them, I represented new hope. I listened intently, jotting down her concerns, when a wail jolted me into the reality of the moment.

Snaking our way through a sea of toys and children to a distant corner, Katherine and I found Victor in a secluded fortress. He sat huddled in his self-imposed prison between the bookshelf and the teachers' reading chair. Face to the wall, Victor's rhythmic rocking silently screamed, "Stay

6

away!" Crouching down from a safe distance, Katherine reached out a gentle hand to him. She leaned toward him awaiting any momentary eye contact or softened response. A hush fell between us. Suddenly hope was dashed as Victor's little shoulders recoiled. Flinging his arms around his belly, he emitted a bitter scream, as tears rolled down his toddler cheeks.

Shaking her head solemnly, Katherine arose to give him more space. We stood quietly waiting for him to calm down. Katherine bit her lip and folded her arms across her broad chest which had comforted hundreds of children. As Victor quieted, with my encouragement, Katherine stooped down and carefully gathered him into her lap. She enfolded him in a tender embrace; but her humming and rocking only triggered Victor to wiggle and writhe, making another escape to seclusion.

Rising to her feet she lamented once again, "We just don't know what to do." Katherine and I shared a knowing that we had an uphill trek ahead of us.

Glancing up in thoughtful reflection, I gently encouraged, "I can tell you that there are strategies which may help. I will do all I can…" *with God's help, inspired revelation and lots of prayer*, I thought to myself. 'Oh dear Lord, encounter this boy with your love and heal him,' I prayed silently as I walked down the stone corridor of the old school building. 'Dear God, give us your wisdom and grace to help this child.'

The following week, I worked with Victor applying every therapeutic strategy I had learned over many years in the field. They had helped so many before him, even with similar diagnosis. But weeks passed and nothing changed. We tried to lead him into comfortable safe experiences where he could begin to engage and connect. In the end, he remained encased in an unreachable secret world of distress. No eye contact, no interaction, no smiles, only tears and inner chaos persisted. I was stumped. I prayed and prayed some more.

In desperation, I gravitated to my new friend at the school. I knocked on Charlie's door to join him for a break. I noted his well-worn sign on his door: JANITOR, thinking he sure is far more than a maintenance man to me. A good twenty years my senior, I was growing to rely on him as a wise counselor and pal. He was becoming a faithful friend who'd helped me fix therapy equipment or creatively adapt a toy for a child.

"Ooh, I think we can take care of that for ya, missy," Charlie would say. "Don't you be worrying about a thing," teasing me carefully about a tendency to fret, I had inherited from my mom.

I relaxed around Charlie. Anxiety and overwhelm in the face of extraordinary needs of my patients coupled with a tendency to take on too much responsibility had been my downfall for years. A gentle smile would curl across Charlie's face as he draped a muscular fatherly arm across my shoulder.

"It's gonna be all right. We'll get 'er done." Often with a tag line of "this afternoon okay?" I'd heave an audible sigh through a grateful smile and check one more thing off my extensive 'to do' list.

Our exchanges which began as a seeking of quick solutions to therapeutic equipment needs evolved into extended break time discussions. I sought his reflections from his pure heart for the children and his respect for the teachers. A monument at the school after 16 years of faithful service, Charlie's insights about children and staff streamlined my perspectives.

In more recent discussions, this eternally happy man had begun to share his relationship with Jesus and faith in His healing power. I wondered how many prayers were going up from that custodian's room. I reflected on the numerous moments I'd observed him gently patting a child's shoulder smiling and giving an encouraging word. I now was certain most encounters were accompanied by a silent prayer. The children flocked to him. They knew he loved them. I felt loved too. We all trusted Charlie.

"I am really concerned about Victor, Charlie. You know the little one in Katherine's preschool program?" I pulled up a stool Charlie kept for visitors.

"Oh yes, little Victor." He leaned back in his swivel chair to gaze up. He looked into the tall cathedral ceiling stuffed with a myriad of boxes of tools and maintenance supplies. I starred at his massive but solid frame and fixated on his strong ebony face. I was hoping to catch a glimpse of some hidden secret he knew about Victor that would unlock this very confounding case. Looking for a key, I waited.

"What do you see, Charlie? I'm about at my wits end. Victor's so unhappy and the teachers can't take much more."

Silence persisted. I tried to wait. Charlie lowered his gaze to look at the floor. I had never asked before, but I blurted out, "Would you go with me to pray over him Charlie? Maybe, maybe our prayers together...." I stopped and waited again, concerned I had asked too much.

Leaning his big body forward to rest his arms on his knees, he folded his hands solemnly. Time passed. Then looking up, "Sure, honey, I can pray with you."

Bursting with new faith, I exclaimed, "Lunch is happening right now. This could be a good time to catch him!" Charlie's shoulders rocked as he chuckled, "Well that would be just fine, yes, just fine." He rose to tackle the job at hand.

In my typical fervor, not wanting to lose momentum, I nearly ran out of Charlie's office. He leisurely trailed, his long lumbering legs propelling him forward in confidence. I hustled through the wooden double doors of the lunchroom and stopped short.

9

Hmmm....where's Victor? I thought to myself. He wasn't in his seat.

A screech echoing off the brick cafeteria walls and a racing teacher hot on the trail of a boy at the far end of the room, answered my question. Katherine smiled gratefully as she slowed her gait in my approach. We corralled Victor, reined him back to his lunch table and guided him into his chair.

Victor gripped the edge of the table, pushing back with heroic strength against our attempt to slide his chair. Gently but firmly I positioned him, knowing we only had moments before another eruption would catapult him into his next frenzy. Charlie's peaceful brown eyes smiled toward mine bringing calm to my spirit. Then as though Charlie had practiced hundreds of well-scripted rehearsals, he rested a gigantic fatherly hand on Victor's tiny shoulder. An exaggerated deep breath from Charlie forced my worried mind into submission and drew my beleaguered heart to attend to Jesus. Charlie smiled confidently in an upward gaze at something or someone. His lips moved silently. I was close enough to hear whispered praises to a God of healing and love. I joined him, grateful to have a mighty prayer partner.

As we waited and prayed for a moment, Victor's body stilled. Under my hand, to my shock and surprise I felt his tiny shoulder soften from its usual rigid vigilant state. His head bowed down slightly and his little chest and arms relaxed. He leaned forward. Victor's entire upper frame was now resting against the table's edge completely still with his hands resting in his lap. Two minutes passed as we continued to pray. Time seemed quickened, yet somehow slowed, hard to explain. I heard a long deep sigh from Victor's lips.

Then this child who had never made direct eye contact with anyone, including his mom by her sad report, this child who had never smiled in his entire three years of life, stunned us all. He turned his little body in his chair directly toward me. He flashed a toothy sweet smile as he looked long and deep into my eyes. He then twisted in his chair to smile directly at Charlie. I watched Charlie's face unfold into a broad grin. He nodded slowly at Victor, almost like he was welcoming him back to the real world. I saw Charlie's lips mouth, "Thank you Jesus."

Then Victor turned forward again to bring his full attention to his plate of spaghetti in front of him. He enthusiastically picked up his spoon and without any help or prompting, spoonful by spoonful, he finished off his entire plate of spaghetti. Then, to our amazement, he cleaned his entire cup of applesauce.

The teachers blinked wildly. With speechless mouths gapping, Katherine, her aide, Charlie and I starred at a completely transformed child. A stir was signaled around the table. Something incredible had just happened, but was it possible? A small uncontrollable leap landed me in Charlie's arms, embracing his huge chest.

Charlie and I stood arm in arm through the end of the lunch period, like proud parents. Then as if we had not witnessed enough, we watched Victor happily take Katherine's hand to be led peacefully back to class. We gleamed together as we watched this sweet natured boy follow like a practiced chick behind his mother hen so glad now, it seemed, to be a beloved part of the flock.

Charlie and I stole away to his office. As I danced around his 100 square foot office praising God and subduing yelps to Jesus, I exploded, "Isn't God good!"

With his usual steadfast candor, yet wiping a wet eye, Charlie drawled, "All the time, Miss Anita, all the time!"

That very afternoon, Katherine and I stood in her classroom, shaking our heads in awe, as we watched little Victor interact with the other children. We watched spellbound as he leaned over the children's activity table, while he carefully placed large wooden puzzle pieces into a board with ease. Then he stunned us still further as we watched him reach out his little arm pointing his finger to each child around the table. Grinning, one by one he spontaneously pointed to and named his classmates. "Mary!" he exclaimed. Then pointing to another, "Sam!" and again with exuberance, "Katie."

I could only wonder how happy Victor's little spirit was to be freed up by the grace of God, to be released from prison, now free to connect with his little friends. Apparently, even from his prison gate, he had been retaining information in preparation for this day of freedom.

Three days later, while I was working with another child in the cafeteria, a woman approached me, straddled a nearby chair across from me and said,

"Hi, I'm Beth, Victor's speech therapist. Are you, Anita his occupational therapist?"

"Yes, I am. Nice to meet you," I answered.

"I just wanted to talk with you about Victor for a minute," she continued. "Do you know what happened to him? He's like a completely different kid!"

I smiled. "Yes, he's doing well isn't he?" Silently thanking Jesus but also asking God silently, *how am I to explain this dramatic shift?* Healing prayer and its results were not written up in the standard school protocol.

Then more insistent, she pressed on, "Yes, but I mean, through our entire 30 minute session, he did everything I gave him. He stayed on task the whole time. I usually have to grab him every 20 to 30 seconds to try to keep him in his seat."

Looking up from my treatment, I smiled. Glad to hear more confirmation of how well Victor was doing, but not knowing what else to say, I remained silent and prayed.

"I mean it, I timed him." she continued, pointing to her stopwatch hanging from her therapy bag. "During his session, I could just keep changing activities and he did great every time."

"I know, I know. It's so good isn't it?" I responded sincerely, but I knew I was just buying time.

"Yeah, yeah, but I mean he's like a normal 3 yr. old!" Beth nearly shouted now. Then she cracked open the real question: "I hear you're doing some kind of different therapy. What is it?"

I responded simply, "Well, prayer always helps."

She nodded smiling, "Of course, of course, but what are you doing with him?"

I tried to deflect her line of questioning, but I could see her astonishment was pressing her forward. I shared some general thoughts on using rocking and sensory techniques, but finally I just reiterated "and, like I said, prayer helps."

She walked away obviously confounded, but I knew it was not the moment to share the full truth, not the time or the season. I just prayed that God would open the door for me to share more at another time if He so desired. I knew Beth and I would soon be able to discharge Victor from our caseloads, as he was sky-rocketing into normal function for a 3-year-old. Truly amazing!

An entire year later, I happened to be invited by a friend to attend a Christian concert at a local church. To my complete surprise, Beth appeared on stage as one of the performers, singing beautiful Christian songs. I was shocked. I had a sense God had set up this divine appointment. I made it a point to go backstage, after the concert. After offering kudos for her fine performance, I launched in.

"Say, Beth do you remember when we worked with a child named Victor over at Clairmont School? There's more to the story. Wanna hear it?"

She was eager to hear. Telling her the story of how God moved on Victor in the lunchroom that day was a precious event to share. At first, she was stunned and then moved to tears.

"I always wondered, I always wondered," she kept repeating. As she probed further and asked questions, I could see the Lord inspiring her to pray for children with new conviction and faith. We met together over lunch the following week for deeper discussion. I sensed it shifted the way she viewed her work as a speech therapist.

Three years later Sarah, Victor's mom and Katherine both reported that Victor continued to thrive as a normal happy interactive boy, such a dramatic change from his early beginnings. That school, the staff and everyone who knew Victor and Sarah were touched by our God of mercy and grace. God be glorified for His love that reached out and set one of His little ones free!

REFLECTIONS:

Partnering in agreement with another in prayer multiplies faith and power. We are promised that if two agree on earth for anything, it will be done by our Father in heaven. In this very challenging situation, I needed someone to stand in prayer with me. Victor was bound by an infirmity of his body, mind, will and emotions from which his merciful Father in heaven wanted to free him. In seeing Victor's torment, his mother, teachers, Charlie and me, all shared a desperate desire to see this child find relief and freedom. In our fervent desperation for God's mercy, our prayers were potent. When needed, we can ask God to show us His heart of mercy for a person, so we can pray with deeper compassion.

The Lord was also drawing both Victor's teachers and his speech therapist, Beth into a greater revelation of God's desire and power to set prisoners free. Waiting on the timing of God is often crucial for God's greater purposes to come forth. I grew to understand there are specific times and seasons for particular moves of God. In retrospect, I could see God's perfect timing in Beth and me sharing at a later meeting. Through it, He received the greatest glory and she was most deeply impacted and transformed. God is always looking to bless at the highest level for the highest good.

SCRIPTURES:

Matthew 18:19 Again I say to you that if two of you agree on earth concerning anything that they ask, it will be done for them by My Father in heaven. NKJV

Isaiah 61:1 The Spirit of the Lord God is upon Me, Because the Lord has anointed Me, To preach good tidings to the poor; He has sent Me to heal the brokenhearted, To proclaim liberty to the captives, And opening of the prison to those who are bound. NKJV

James 5:15, 16: And the prayers of faith will save the sick and Lord will raise him up. And if he has committed sins, he will be forgiven. Confess your trespasses to one another and pray for one another, that you may be healed. The effective, fervent prayers of a righteous man avails much. NKJV

Ecclesiastes 3:1: To everything there is a season, A time for every season under heaven. NKJV

3

HOPE FOR BRAIN INJURY

I watched from the bay window as she approached the house. Sandra's left leg and foot dragged behind her. It seemed so unfair for an 11-year-old to have to work so hard just to walk. Her drooping left arm showed the evidence of her violent catapult through the windshield the year before. I saw her struggle up the stairs toward the door. Carol, her mom had been standing with me filling me in on more of the story.

"The auto wreck changed every part of her life, Anita. And mine for that matter. It all happened so fast....I can still hear her scream as she flew out of the car. Why wasn't it me...?" Her voice trailed off as she brushed a tear and cleared her throat just as Sandra reached for the door.

Carol and I had been talking for about a half hour and my notes from the medical chart concurred; Sandra's diagnosis of Severe Traumatic Brain Injury devastated this once vibrant pre-teen. Desperately the family had hung onto hope that she might return to normal. It had been so long now, though... Carol said she felt that people were giving up. The pause in the conversation begged the question. *'Could I still help? Was there hope for change?'*

Sandra let the screen door slam behind her sending a fierce shudder through the house. Mom winced a bit but then recovered to say,

"Try to remember, Sandra, to come in the house quietly, sweetie. Thank you."

Sandra stood a few feet away from me as we greeted. But then she abruptly blurted, "Will my eyes ever get better?" Her question ended in a shrill high pitch. I could see she was straining to focus on me through her crossed eyes and double vision. I reached out taking her hand gently saying, "We'll just keep doing your exercises and we'll see. You're doing great." I had clearly not given up, but I knew options were rapidly deteriorating. I was praying regularly and seeking wisdom and the counsel of God. *How much do I encourage? How much do I prepare her for the worst?*, I wondered.

Sandra turned away from me and took off running. Her brunette bob flipped across her shoulders as she bolted past Mary, her sister. "Shut up! Stop buggin' me!" Sandra screamed as she ran past her sibling. Mary looked from me to her mom, bewildered, shrugging her shoulders as if to say, "What did I do?"

"It's okay, honey." Carol reassured in a hushed tone. Carol motioned Mary toward her on the couch. Wrapping her large strong arms around Mary, Carol drew her younger daughter to her bosom tenderly, "It's nothing you did. She's just havin' a bad day."

"Again?!" shot back Mary. "I wish she'd just stop it!"

Carol maneuvered her round frame to the edge of the couch, pushing herself up, expelling a gasp with a slight cough. She reached out a comforting hand and led Mary to the far end of the room. Their whispered interchange was an obvious attempt by Carol to try to bridge a chasm that was eroding a once deep bond between her two girls. With a smile and kiss on her forehead, Carol sent Mary to grab a treat and go off to play in her room. Carol sank deeply back into the couch with a groan.

"Looks like it's been real challenging for all of you," I said.

"It's a cruel metamorphosis, Anita." Carol stared blankly at the wall. "Those two girls were inseparable, best friends. Sandra was the original 'big sis,' always lookin' out for Mary. The doctors say she's reverted to a seven-year-old, a very emotional and unhappy seven-year-old, I might add." Carol's shoulders slumped now. Her arms lay limp at her sides, as she stared at the carpet at some imaginary screen playing back memories. "Racing bikes to the park with Mary after homework and dishes every day. THAT'S what I remember. Now anytime I ask Sandra to do the smallest thing, she just screams, 'I don't want to!' and runs and hides. I barely recognize her."

Nodding I offered, "It must be so difficult to see all the changes."

"And lately all she talks about are her eyes. Then she cries. It makes her so sad. Carol gazed out the window caught up once again, it seemed by a glimpse and longing for the past. "She asks me to pray every night for God to heal her eyes."

I knew that the other team members were beginning to teach the family coping strategies readying them for discharge. I clearly didn't have the answer to these massive questions. I committed to myself to pray more about this.

Then Tuesday arrived just two weeks later. A normal visit started like any other. Sandra teetered on the rocker board balancing on her knees as her arms and hands stretched out to catch the air borne bean bags.

"Oh, almost – good try! Yes, that's it! Good catch!" I encouraged.

Then as one of the red vinyl bags lofted mid-air between us, I sensed an inner vision, a quick but most vivid impression of Sandra looking straight at me with healthy eyes. In this picture in my mind's eye, she no longer had turned in eyes, but she was looking straight ahead, both eyes strong and healthy. It was exciting! I knew from experience, that when God gave me a glimpse of someone healed, He was showing me what had already been planned in heaven for them. He just needed someone to agree in Jesus' name to manifest it on the earth.

As if someone behind me was speaking, I heard myself saying to Sandra and Carol, "I believe God wants to heal your eyes, Sandra. Do you want to pray together to ask Him for that?"

I was surprised by my own boldness and strength of my conviction, but I had learned to trust those impressions from the Lord. Both Carol and Sandra in unison stepped toward me with eager anticipation. I placed one of my hands over Sandra's eyes as we agreed in prayer.

"Oh God, in the mighty name of Jesus Christ, we agree and thank you for bringing forth the fullness of Sandra's eyes being healed in Jesus' name." Carol whispered her thanks to God as she nodded in agreement. Sandra closed with "Thank you, Jesus." As I drove away from their house that day, I felt a peace that we had prayed God's true heart.

Now what I had not known was that her ophthalmologist, Dr. Hanlon, had scheduled Sandra for cosmetic eye surgery just five days after that prayer session. This procedure surgically shortens the eye muscles which pulls the eyes into alignment. If the surgery is successful, it allows the eyes a chance to work better together. The surgery is not a solution but rather a step in the long process of on-going treatment, primarily a cosmetic adjustment. On the day she was to have surgery, I received a most stunning phone call at work from a stuttering and ecstatic Carol. I was not prepared for what I heard.

"We got up, just this morning. I walked into her room to wake her up...to, to tell her to get ready for her surgery appointment...and, and Anita, she looked up at me and, she was looking straight at me! Her eyes were straight and she could see normal, no double vision! She kept looking in the mirror and running around the house so excited!"

Carol paused waiting for my response, but I was speechless other than a stunned, "Oh my goodness." I was grateful for the sturdy wooden arms of the office chair right behind me. I grabbed it and eased myself down.

She continued. "I almost called the clinic to cancel our appointment but then I figured we better go ahead. So we went in. They examined her and Dr. Hanlon checked her. He even called in two other docs and they all agreed. She has no double vision. Her eyes are perfectly normal! They cancelled the surgery and sent us home!"

I managed to ask: "How's Sandra feeling?"

"Oh, she is so-o-o happy! Wait 'til you see her."

The following week, I visited Sandra at her school. I slammed my car door behind me and trudged across hot asphalt. From a distance, I caught a glimpse of her class on the playground. Squinting to see against the blazing sun, I crossed the sidewalk to the gate.

My fingers gripped the metal fencing, in part to steady myself. Peering through the crisscross meshing, I stood mesmerized. Could that be Sandra? Why certainly it was! I gawked as she courageously climbed to the top of the high monkey bars, 10 feet above ground with her buddies, Patty and Susie. Amid the din of recess chaos, I heard "Sandra, try this!" and "Do this, Sandra!" Their voices echoed above peels of laughter and squeals. Sandra gleefully responded.

No longer was she exiled to the bench below, to watch longingly. Today she climbed and chimed in with her friends with new boldness and freedom. My hands clung to the wire fence fixated on this wondrous beginning of a life restored. I could see that her maneuvering favored that weaker left side but her whole body was engaged at an entirely new level. Every swing, every pivot, every challenge was building new strength and new stamina. Eyes moist now, I whispered, "Thank you, Jesus."

Sandra's mountaintop healing journey, however, was still beset with valleys to be traversed. "She shouts out and interrupts all day long!" said Sandra's 4th grade teacher, Ms. Riley. She released a wave of frustration as she vented to me in the hallway at her school. "No matter how many consequences I give her, nothing works. She just can't settle down! I think she needs meds or something. She's way behind on all her assignments." The frazzled teacher went on. "The child simply cannot stay in her seat, interrupting, sharpening pencils. It's disruptive to the whole class. We've got to have a team conference and I WILL be recommending a psychiatric assessment!"

I was troubled leaving the school that day. Sandra had come so far, but would this be her nemesis? Would we win the battle but lose the war by having some behavioral drug introduced? There were often so many side effects from drugs. I needed to discuss this issue with Carol and Sandra. "Oh, Lord – give me wisdom and bring healing for Sandra," I prayed silently as I tugged open the heavy wooden door leaving Forbes Elementary.

Huddled together on the living room floor two days later, Carol, Sandra and I sat cross-legged leaning in toward one another. We had to speak quietly. Mary was in the next room taking a nap.

"Sweetie, do you know that you can't speak out in class? You know that Ms. Riley doesn't want you to get up to sharpen your pencils or talk to friends, right? Did you know she needs you to stop that?" I asked Sandra.

"I know...I know." Tears were now rolling down her lovely flushed cheeks. I hated to cause this but I had to know if she understood the teacher's expectations.

"Have you tried to change and do things differently?" I gently asked.

"Yeah, but…."

"But what, honey?" I coaxed.

"I can't stop. It just keeps happening."

Carol and I exchanged a pained look to one another, struck by Sandra's sincerity and candor. Then I lowered my head, pausing and getting a sense we needed to pray. "Sandra, do you remember how Jesus helped you with your eyes?" I asked.

Her tears subsided now as she sniffed and wiped her dripping nose with her shirt sleeve. She looked up at me nodding and then glanced over to her mom.

"Shall we ask Him for help again?" I cautiously inquired.

She nodded her head enthusiastically. I reached for Carol's hand and we all followed suit. "Lord Jesus, bring peace and focus to Sandra's mind. Help her with attending to her assignments in her classroom. Lord, please help with her behavior and showing respect for her teacher, in Jesus' name we pray."

It was a simple prayer but we felt the peace and presence of the Spirit of God fall in the room and we lingered in the stillness.

As we closed the prayer, Sandra showed her unabashed trust in God saying, "Thank you for helping me."

I sensed a leading in my spirit to also teach Sandra a prayer, a simple prayer to repeat silently during class. I demonstrated how to take deep breaths saying, "Jesus" (on the in-breath) and "help me" (on the out-breath). After practicing with me, she promised to try this at school.

Two weeks passed since we had prayed together. I arrived at the school and searched for her teacher. Ms. Riley's classroom aide directed me down a long hall and into a staff lounge. Ms. Riley, seeing me enter, invited me into to an adjacent room. With her hands on her hips she looked down, expelled a long deep breath, shook her head and said, "I think it's been about the past seven days or so. She's really been calm." Now nodding, confirming her thoughts to herself, "She's focused on her work and getting a lot done."

Then our eyes meeting, she was apparently struck by the dramatic difference from our last conversation, "Well", she huffed a breath of near disbelief, "I sure hope it lasts."

Silently praising God, I just chimed in, "I'm with you on that!" We smiled together and parted.

Leaving Ms. Riley, I passed Sandra in the hallway on her way to the lunchroom. "Say, Sandra sweetie, how are you doing? I just spoke with your teacher and she told me she's really pleased with how calm and focused you've been in class and about all the good work you're getting done."

"Yeah! I'm almost all caught up on my assignments!"

"Do you think Jesus is helping you again?" I asked.

Smiling she nodded saying, "I do that thing you taught me."

I learned later that without my knowing, Ms. Riley had requested a referral for a behavioral specialist to come into her classroom to do a clinical assessment on Sandra which began with a classroom observation. The specialist had been delayed with a busy schedule. In the interim, Ms. Riley had not had time to inform the specialist of the changes she had been seeing in Sandra; so the behavioral specialist entered the classroom searching for this 'very disruptive, impulsive child' that had been described to her previously.

The specialist explained to me later. "I tucked myself into one of the desks in the room assuming this child would be very obvious to me. I was certain that though we had not met, from the description of her erratic abnormal behavior, I would have no trouble identifying her. Well, when I couldn't find anyone fitting this description, I finally asked Ms. Riley to point Sandra out to me."

The behavioral specialist's account later read, "I found Sandra to be one of the most productive and focused students in the room."

One year later during a follow-up staffing with Carol and me attending, the team leader read in the summary report that "Sandra has sustained normal function" and was actually "ranking above the norm in productivity, attention and overall academic performance." This concluded the amazing testimony with the medical team report which read "no residual symptoms from her severe traumatic brain injury."

As Carol hugged me that day at the close of the meeting, she took me aside to say, "Thanks for never giving up. Thanks for trusting Jesus and listening to Him." I reminded her that it was her prayers and her faith in God's healing and deliverance that made all the difference. Carol and I slung our arms around one another's waists as we walked down the hallway from that meeting. As we strolled together, we watched Mary and Sandra race up ahead together. They wanted to get in one last turn on the playground swings before heading home to ride their bikes to the park.

REFLECTIONS:

Jesus taught that He only did what His Father in heaven showed him He was doing. Jesus is our model; so I make it a regular practice in healing prayer, to begin by asking to be shown what the Father is doing. I may sense in my spirit through an impression or an actual picture or vision what is on the Father's heart that's already being done or has been done in the heavenly realm. That prayer for direction or insight is not always answered immediately, but may be an impression that comes over time.

When I sense clear direction, as to how to specifically pray, I step out in faith. I agree and pray in accordance with what I sense is in alignment with the Father's heart and will from heaven. I do what Jesus did. He said He does nothing of His own accord, but only what His Father in heaven is doing. Then I pray to my Father in heaven through the power of Jesus' blood that was shed on the cross through the power of the Holy Spirit for that healing or deliverance. Of course, this is with the full knowing that Jesus bore our sicknesses, diseases, grief and sorrow and that by His stripes, the lashes He took upon His body as our sacrificial Lamb, we can be healed. That is our promise.

I often ask the person being prayed for if they want this healing or can agree for this healing. Jesus trusted in the Father for His sovereign move of His heart and hand for His beloved children. Jesus however often said, "your faith has made you whole," so it seems clear that inviting agreement in prayer engages their faith and can be essential in seeing healing come forth.

Jesus said to pray, "Thy Kingdom come, Thy Will be done, on earth AS it is in heaven." In heaven there are only perfected bodies. There is no illness or infirmity there. We can call on the Truth that He went to the cross, took the keys from the kingdom of darkness and has dominion over death and destruction. By His Name, we also can stand in the authority of Jesus to see healing for today. What Christ did on the cross 2000 years ago establishes our right to be healed and delivered and set free today.

SCRIPTURES:

Luke 11:2   So He said to them, "When you pray, say: Our Father in heaven, Hallowed be your name. Your kingdom come. Your will be done on earth as it is in heaven." NKJV

John 5:19-20 Then Jesus answered and said to them, "Most assuredly, I say to you, the Son can do nothing of Himself, but what He sees the Father do; for whatever He does, the Son also does in like manner. For the Father loves the Son, and shows Him all things that He Himself does; and He will show Him greater works than these, that you may marvel." NKJV

Luke 18:41-43 (Jesus) saying, "What do you want me to do for you?" He said, "Lord that I may receive my sight." Then Jesus said to him, "Receive your sight; your faith has made you well." And immediately he received his sight, and followed Him. And the people, when they saw it, gave praise to God. NKJV

4

PROVIDENCE FOR PARKINSONS

Entering Crescent Manor, a skilled nursing facility, I stopped to chat with a nurse. Glancing over her shoulder as we spoke, I could see 82-year-old Fred Allen shuffling down the hallway with his walker. His full body tremors were increasing as he picked up speed. That was the Parkinson's disease. His escalating rapid pace and darting eyes were scary to watch from a distance. I pointed, alerting my colleague and then took off, hurrying to give him a hand. It was too late. Before I could reach him, he became a weaving vortex of motion, walker flying out from under him. Fred sadly lay in a heap halfway down the hall. My heart sank as I saw humiliation and despair sweep over his face as aides gathered him with soothing words of encouragement. Miraculously, other than a few bruises, Fred was not seriously injured. However, his grieved countenance reflected his fear of dependency in his future.

Reports of these sudden spills were increasing in recent weeks. As he attempted the short trek from his bed to his bathroom, his quaking unsteadiness was upsetting his wife, Cecile, who shared his room. Fred wasn't waiting for an aide to help him, so many falls were happening as he bolted to his bathroom in their private room. Cecile's panicked screams could be heard echoing down the hallway.

"Please help my husband," she would shout to anyone passing by. Her pleas had recently been drawing me into their room. It worried me. My visits often turned into supportive chats. I liked them. Cecile appeared overwhelmed and stressed, but considering all that she was dealing with, it seemed reasonable. I enjoyed Fred's wry sense of humor which brought a bit of comic relief to a difficult situation. A bond was growing between us.

Several weeks later, I was called in on the case. On my first day, I got word that his doctor had decided to restrict Fred to walk with his walker under supervision only. Maneuvering himself around the facility on his own seemed like a thing of the past. Though a necessary medical call, this decision plunged Fred into an even deeper state of hopelessness and despair.

I started Fred on a rather aggressive therapeutic program that often brought swift change for my patients. It was a specialized treatment that had helped other patients to regain balance and steadiness. The procedure was birthed out of a revelation through prayer when I asked God to show me something to help my most challenged patients. He showed me how to include mental imagery coupled with prayer with my usual therapy. So I decided to try it with Fred.

"Let's just have you sit here, Fred, at the side of your bed. First we'll have you simply close your eyes and imagine how it might look and feel to put on your shirt and slip into your pants. Then you'll imagine using your walker, paying close attention to the details of your movements and subtle rhythmic changes of your body."

He sat on the edge of his bed visualizing. His eyelids fluttered slightly being unfamiliar with purposeful mental imagery.

"Try to imagine putting on your favorite brown trousers. Imagine just sitting on the edge of the bed as you are now, holding the pants around the waist. Then imagine putting in one leg and then the other. Don't actually move, just use your imagination."

"I can do it real easy in my imagination, heh-heh," he chortled.

Cecile smiled. I suspected that she was glad to see some of her husband's natural humor surfacing.

"Okay, first the right leg and then the left," I said trying to keep him focused.

"Now what?" he responded.

"Imagine standing up carefully and slowly pulling your pants up around your waist…now fastening and zipping….Got it?"

"Yeah, now if it was always this easy….." he said smiling.

"Well, that's what we're goin' for Fred. You're doing great," I encouraged.

"So you say the Olympic athletes do this stuff – this imagining thing?" he asked.

"Yes, and with good results! Trust me. Now let's try imagining maneuvering your walker from your bed to your bathroom, just ten short feet. Visualize long slow strides. Feel the rhythm of your gait. Notice you can imagine lifting your head and watching where you're going. This is all a part of the body awareness and motor relearning, feeling it inside before doing it with your physical body."

"Hmmm. I'm imagining rounding the corner heading into the bathroom with my walker, trying to go slow like you said."

"How did that go in your mind's eye, Fred?" I asked.

"Pretty good."

"Okay, now we will have you open your eyes and do everything you just imagined. I will be right here, if you need me."

Cecile watched us, smiling, hopeful for a breakthrough for her husband of 52 years.

"Good honey! I told you Nita could help us," she encouraged.

Frankly, Cecile had much more confidence in me than I did. I had the same concerns as the rest of the staff. Parkinson's being a progressive degenerative disease meant the prognosis was not statistically hopeful.

However, I was noticing that each time we practiced with the imagining, he was more focused and pacing his movements better. Over several weeks, he seemed steadier while he was dressing and walking. Yet I felt quite certain that if left on his own, he would speed up and take a spill. I knew from my past experience with teaching this mental imagery strategy that the real breakthrough came when patients invited Jesus as their partner in healing. But I didn't even know if Fred or Cecile had a belief in God. I felt prompted to simply ask them. We had built a nice rapport so I cautiously broached the subject. As he sat comfortably on his bed across from Cecile, in the privacy of their room, I struck up a conversation about it.

"Say, do you have a spiritual walk? Do you ever pray for help?"

"Not really," Fred responded with a curled lip and blank stare.

I silently prayed that the Lord would make me sensitive to ask the right questions. Hesitantly, I pursued the subject.

"Did you ever go to church when you were young?" I asked.

"Ha!" He looked down, shaking his head. "Didn't have much choice about THAT!"

"What do you mean, Fred?"

I glanced over at Cecile. She looked a little nervous but offered, "Tell her, Fred, go ahead." And while Fred sat silent, she said, "His dad...well, it just wasn't right...what happened....just wasn't right. Come on Fred. Tell her."

"I'll tell you what you can do with RELIGION....it's NOT for me! Yeah, my dad was the preacher. I was what they called a PK!!"

31

"PK, Fred?"

"YEAH, a PREACHER'S KID!" he blurted out. He was obviously very angry and from the sounds of it, with good reason.

"Do you want to tell me about it, Fred? It's up to you. You don't have to, but I'm a pretty good listener."

He glanced up at me, saw my sincerity and concern. We had a fairly good connection by now and that helped.

"Well if I did anything that he didn't think was being a good Christian, he'd get real mad."

"What would he get mad about?"

"Well, I don't even know. One of the first times I got beat was when I was pretty young."

"Beat Fred? How old?" I asked.

I glanced at Cecile. She was shaking her head, tears filling her eyes.

"Go ahead, tell her. He's never told anybody, 'cause he doesn't think he should talk about it," Cecile shared.

Almost in a whisper, he said, "I was probably only four or five the first time."

"Oh Fred, I'm so sorry. You were just a little boy. What happened?" I encouraged him to tell his story. I knew that just speaking the truth out loud can bring healing.

"He told me I was no good. He called me dumb and a bastard, said I'd never amount to anything. Then he beat me with a heavy leather strap. Gave me welts on my legs and arms that would bleed."

Fred's head hung low. It was apparent he still carried emotional wounds from the beatings and the raging accusations. It's so common that the abused child often blames themselves for what happened because throughout the abuse, the abuser blames them. It goes into their minds and hearts so deeply that the victim often carries unwarranted guilt and shame for years.

"Oh my goodness, Fred. I am so sorry that happened to you."

"Well, I was kind of a rebellious kid and then I was no angel when I grew up. I probably deserved it."

Cecile looked down and then out the window. She tensed and I perceived there was a whole story there.

"Fred, I imagine that you did rise up to try and defend yourself at times. Maybe even yelled back, but that would be a normal response for that situation. That's not being rebellious. What could a little boy have done that would warrant a beating with a thick leather belt, that left bloody welts on your legs and arms?"

I waited. He sat staring at the floor, pondering my words. Finally after a long silence, he breathed a long deep sigh and continued.

"He drank a lot but who am I to accuse. I drank heavy too." He glanced up at Cecile who looked away again.

"Tell me more about your childhood with your dad, if you can, Fred." I coaxed.

"He was ALL PIOUS on Sundays in front of his d--- church. Then he'd FLY INTO A RAGE and BEAT US at home. Yeah, you can take the church and SHOVE IT, as far as I'm concerned."

Healthy anger was surfacing. I was relieved. I sensed it was important for him to have a safe place to get this out. Fred shared painful anguished memories of beatings and the torment of watching his younger brother scream and cry under the cruelty of his dad's belt. He shared the remorse and guilt of wanting to stand up for his sibling, but so scared, he hid instead.

Feelings surfaced that had been buried for decades. His father presented himself to his church as a kind and patient servant of the Lord, then morphed into an alcohol-driven, raging man at home which left wounds of distrust and resentment. Most painfully, Fred got in touch with the fact that his dad had beaten him for the minor infractions of a rambunctious little boy. A most touching part of the story was where he recalled that he'd invited Jesus into his heart as a pre-teen and prayed regularly. However because of the abuse, his belief in a loving God was virtually shattered.

"I walked away from religion and the Lord," he explained, "then I started drinking a lot." He further confessed to me, through deep shame and remorse that he ended up beating Cecile, carrying on his dad's legacy of brutality. I suddenly saw Cecile's pain and anxiety from a whole new vantage point.

I could sense the Lord's heart of compassion, mercy and forgiveness toward this tortured man. We discussed the inevitable mix of feelings after suffering at the hands of a confused and deceived parent. As we spoke, you could almost see the layers of fear and shame melt off of him. He was a shell of a man that housed a little boy inside who so needed to know the kindness of a loving father.

"Fred, would you allow me to just pray for you right now?" I asked.

In this atmosphere of truth and potential freedom, he said, "Sure," as he bowed his head.

I led him in a prayer asking Jesus to comfort and heal the deep wounds and memories from his past. We also asked the heavenly Father to remove the spiritual darts of critical abusive words and actions that pierced Fred's heart. We asked for those wounded places in his soul to be replaced with God's healing balm of Love. The Lord graciously met Fred with a manifestation of God's presence of love, peace and joy.

Tenderized by the love and kindness of God, he repented for his own mistakes he'd made in his life and the abuse he perpetrated on Cecile in their marriage. Through prayer, we finally loosed Satan's strongholds from Fred in these areas of his life in the name of Jesus Christ.

The Holy Spirit's presence was palpable in the room. A deep peace was visible on Fred's face as he renewed his connection with Jesus, reviving his relationship with God as he saw Jesus was still there loving him and not rejecting him. He could see that Jesus did not desire that he should be so terribly wounded as a child. He also saw that Jesus hated religion too, being reminded that Jesus condemned the Pharisees who were hard on His beloved people. Fred encountered the personal God and friend he had in Jesus who he came to understand, loved him, did not condemn him but rather forgave him and was there to help him even in these latter years of his life.

"Fred, it's been a long time, but Jesus and Father God still want to help you be set free from your past and find peace in Him. Will you invite Him to enter your heart again to help you start receiving the fullness of His grace and peace?"

"Yes," he responded.

"Can I lead you in a short prayer?"

"Please."

He repeated as I led him in prayer, "Jesus, you know everything. You've seen everything. I ask you now to help me. Come into my heart and lead me, direct my path. I ask you to forgive me for anything I may have done in thought, word or deed that did not please you. I thank you for forgiving me and I receive your forgiveness now. I invite you into my life as Savior and Lord, in Jesus' name. Amen."

The witness of the presence of the Lord was weighty in the room. I could see that though Cecile sat quietly in her bed with her head bowed, she had whispered her own prayer in agreement.

"Fred, I want you to ask the Lord a key question that may help you. Are you willing to do that?"

"Yes," he responded.

"Ask the Lord, 'what happened to my dad that caused him to treat me this way?' Just ask and then wait. Try not to figure it out…just ask and wait."

He did. And then with closed eyes, he waited. A minute or so passed and suddenly Fred gasped. He clutched his mouth and then draped a trembling hand over tearful eyes. His head bowed. He wept.

"What is it, Fred?" I asked.

"I never knew….I never knew…."

"What?" I encouraged him to speak the truth out loud to bring freedom.

"I see my dad getting beat up by grandpa…hit him with a belt… then locked in a closet. He was so young." Tears streamed as he shook his head with this new revelation.

"Could this be true? Am I just making this up?" he asked.

"Fred, it is my experience over and over that the Lord so wants us free that He reveals truth that only He could uncover to our hearts and minds."

I felt sad for Fred, yet relieved because I knew that once the common thread in the family line was revealed, there could be great freedom. What is modeled and perpetrated in one generation in a family is so often handed down to the next. Hurting people hurt people.

Thanking me as I left that day, Fred paused and gripped my hand in deep appreciation. A glow shone from his smiling elder face. He looked younger somehow. A knowing passed between us that something profound and life changing had occurred. Something in his heart had shifted. We drew Cecile into this new reality as she rested on her bed. Knowing that though the truth was that she had been a recipient of the drinking and raging of Fred's father and grandfather, new possibilities were on the horizon for her as well. The Holy Spirit's countenance beamed through Fred's aged beatific face as we said our goodbyes that day.

I did not know what the Lord was planning on doing, but I had learned to look forward to His surprises. When I arrived at the rest home two days later, I was greeted by the social worker who asked me excitedly,

"Have you seen Mr. Allen yet?"

Without waiting for my answer, she blurted out with widened eyes,

"He's been walking all over the facility with his walker, with no help from anyone!" Overjoyed to share such good news, she went on, "Yesterday, he pushed Cecile in the wheelchair to the dining room for lunch. You should have seen how proud he looked." Until that day, that wheelchair had been used exclusively for him to be wheeled around in because of his own needs.

"He seems clearer. He looks straight at you when he talks. He just seems happy!" she exclaimed.

The staff was in a flurry, each one reporting various versions of stories expressing their amazement at this sudden and dramatic change in Mr. Allen. They wanted me to help them to understand what had happened. Many of the staff were prayerful believers in the miracle workings of God and were open to hearing that it was the Lord Jesus' grace that healed Fred. Others just remained awed, but seeds of hope and truth were planted all over the facility that day.

Later that day, Fred and Cecile's son, Phillip approached me with an extended hand of gratitude. Phillip had been the one son who remained a faithful supporter of his parents. He was obviously excited about the changes in his dad and asked what had happened. I shared the process of prayer ministry that his father received. Phillip was grateful for God's inner healing that led to his father's physical healing.

Phillip enthusiastically asked for my agreement to contact the doctor to try to remove the walking restrictions from his father's chart. The physician, of course, needed to see Mr. Allen to verify the reported sudden improvement in function. A doctor's appointment was arranged through the nursing staff. When the doctor tested and observed Mr. Allen's stability and mental clarity, though surprised by the sudden and dramatic changes, he removed all restrictions. Fred was allowed to use his walker independently without supervision and was given freedom to walk anywhere in or around the facility on his own.

Over the next months, Fred remained physically steady and mentally clear. He learned to take care of his personal needs without help. He continued to walk freely, taking strolls in the gardens around the facility using his walker safely and happily. Most striking was that it was apparent he felt certain of his place in the Lord.

The Lord later inspired me to lead a number of discussions between Fred and Cecile to help them heal the wounds from the abuse in their relationship. They acknowledged their respective mistakes and asked for forgiveness from one another to heal past wounds. We then prayed together for the Lord's blessing on their marriage.

During prayer, the Holy Spirit showed me a picture of Fred and Cecile dancing together. I decided to ask them about it.

"Hey guys, did you ever dance together?"

Both of them smiled broadly.

"Well yeah, I could shake a leg! That's how we met, at the local dance hall." Fred piped up. He glanced over at Cecile with a cheeky grin.

Cecile flushed a bit and said, "We used to dance a lot. I fell in love with him, dancing in his arms." Fred gleamed. Looking over at Fred, she continued, "Dances with Fred were some of my most cherished memories of our early years together."

I decided to include as some of Fred's final therapy goals, to dance with Cecile in their shared room. A few weeks later, as I was about to discharge Fred on a final visit, I arrived to find Cecile dancing in the middle of their room just for her husband, a private performance.

Fred looked on beaming saying, "You still got it, babe."

The Lord is completely faithful and has a season for every blessing.

REFLECTIONS:

As in the case of Fred Allen, it seemed some of my patients' healing was tied to an underlying issue of unworthiness. Life trauma and shame sometimes results in patients not being able to forgive themselves. When a biological mother or father was unable to give the honoring and love that was due, a breakthrough came when God touched them and they experienced the truth that God still and always had loved them. Whether we fully recall or are aware, we are all adopted children of a loving Father God who always desired to enjoy deep relationship with us. Our Creator breathed life into us. His magnificent heart of love formed us so we would enjoy intimate relationship with Him. There is a place in our hearts that can only be filled by Father God's love and sharing closeness with Him.

Early trauma, some remembered and some suppressed, can manifest as illness and disease in later years. But God can and will intervene and free us when we ask Him for revelation and understanding. In quiet meditative prayer, we can make a powerful request of God to show us things about our past by shining His light and love into our hearts asking to see things through His eyes. Many times, as in Fred's case, people believe lies or distorted truths about themselves because of things people said or did to them, when they were far too young to discern truth about themselves. Then that can become a lens through which we unknowingly continue to view ourselves and life.

We can ask the Lord Jesus to show us what He says is true about us to break off such lies and distortions. Further, God can also reveal to our hearts what happened to others that caused them to treat us as they did. These revelations through the eyes of the mercy of God can allow us to forgive what seemed like the unforgiveable. In prayer, God can touch those memories and free us from the pain and trauma of the past and heal us body, soul and spirit.

SCRIPTURES:

Romans 8:15-17 For you did not receive the spirit of bondage again to fear, but you received the Spirit of adoption by whom we cry out "Abba Father." The Spirit Himself bears witness with our spirit that we are children of God, and if children, then heirs – heirs of God and joint heirs with Christ, if indeed we suffer with Him, that we may also be glorified together. NKJV

Psalm 103: 2-4 Bless the Lord, O my soul, And forget not all His benefits: Who forgives all your iniquities, Who heals all your diseases, Who redeems your life from destruction, Who crowns you with lovingkindness and tender mercies. NKJV

John 8:32 "…And you shall know the truth, and the truth shall make you free." NKJV

Jeremiah 31:3 The Lord has appeared of old to me, saying: "Yes, I have loved you with an everlasting love; Therefore with lovingkindness have I drawn you." NKJV

5

TWO TO TANGO

I clipped down the corridor to my last appointment of the day at Harrison Elementary. Screams suddenly erupted and echoed down the hallway. I jolted. Then I remembered. I took a breath, realizing, it must be Tuesday, the day little Casandra gets her physical therapy. Her therapist was trying to do her job, but it had been a long painful battle.

Two-year-old Casandra was born with Cerebral Palsy. Walking past her elaborate wheelchair from time to time had given me opportunities to adore this beautiful blue-eyed toddler. Sadly, her tiny left arm and leg were somewhat drawn up to her chest because of muscle tightness. I knew her therapists were fighting a time clock to release the tightness and foster enough flexibility that might allow her to crawl and walk one day. From the deafening screams from her therapy room, the battle was still raging.

Frankly I'd been avoiding the scene, finding it hard to watch. Normally I'd scurry past their door. Today my heart was compelled to stop, a prompting from the heart of God, I was sure. As I poked my head around the corner of their room, Casandra's huge tear-filled eyes pierced me.

"Hi! How's it goin' today, guys?" I asked.

Marilyn, the physical therapist, was seated on the floor behind Casandra as her little patient leaned forward against a big therapy ball. Marilyn was struggling to stretch Casandra's tight calf and ankle muscles. Marilyn glanced up. She must have caught the sympathetic tone in my greeting and let her guard down.

"This may be one of the worst yet," she groaned.

Casandra twisted her little frame, swinging a defiant arm toward Marilyn, just barely missing her face. Marilyn arched back, averting the lunge.

"Come on Casandra, just work with me!" Marilyn nearly yelled.

Grunting, Casandra bent her head down and then lurched back violently trying to escape Marilyn's hold on her leg.

Marilyn bristled.

Walking towards them, I asked, "Is she ever calm during treatment?"

"Never!" snapped the frustrated therapist. "She's always like this. I've been with her for six months, twice a week. It's always a struggle. Can't be comforted so I just press through."

"Oh my, that's gotta be hard on both of you," I offered.

"Same way with her last two therapists. They finally gave up and discharged her. This is my worst case. I dread every session."

"Wow, that's tough. I can see that you're fighting the good fight, though," I offered.

"Thanks, but sometimes I wonder…." Marilyn's voice trailed off as she rolled her eyes.

Glancing at my watch, I said, "I am so sorry, but I've got to get to my next appointment. Could I drop by another time when I can stay longer?"

"Sure, anytime. Thanks."

"Bless you in all this." Patting Marilyn on the back, I reached down and gave Casandra a quick hug.

"Hang in there," I said as I headed toward the door. I left for my next appointment saying a silent prayer for them as I went.

The following week I had a break in my schedule, so I took the opportunity to visit again.

"Mind if I join you for a bit?" I said as I peeked around the corner.

"No, not at all. Come in," Marilyn responded warmly.

As I walked through the door, Casandra glanced up revealing a flushed face and swollen red eyes. She leaned over the ball while Marilyn stroked, tapped and manipulated her little leg. I straddled a nearby kid-size wooden chair. Casandra whimpered and then let out a piercing scream, as tears streamed down her cheeks.

Marilyn relaxed her hold on Casandra's leg. Through a deep sigh, she said,

"Kind of three steps forward and two steps back. Pretty bad, but it's gotta get done."

Determined, Marilyn refocused and pressed in. I saw Casandra's tiny frame tense and her face grimace.

I felt in my spirit the Lord's desire to see both of them touched. I was sensing His heart to bring comfort and healing as well as to intervene in this ongoing struggle between them.

Tentatively I broached the subject.

"This must be so painful for her, don't you think? To say nothing of how frustrating and upsetting this must be for you, dealing with her anger and resistance all the time."

"Yeah, she can be a real pill! I've pretty much decided to discharge her to another therapist. Can't take much more."

As they worked together, I felt led to place a hand on weeping Casandra. I said a silent prayer for a release of the pain and rebuked and loosed a spirit of discomfort and chaos away from her.

Though I do pray in faith, what I saw next quite surprised me. Within moments, there was a shift. I could sense that something significant had changed. A peace fell over Casandra. Literally her squirming and resistance transformed to calm before my eyes. Casandra looked up at me. A broad smile washed over her face. Her entire countenance had changed.

A few minutes passed wherein Casandra was simply leaning over the therapy ball not resisting the treatment. Marilyn and I chatted about how Casandra seemed to be a bit more relaxed than usual. I gently laid my hand on Marilyn's shoulder as we spoke. Silently, I prayed for the Holy Spirit to wash over Marilyn with His deep peace while loosing spirits of strife and frustration from her. Marilyn's shoulders visibly relaxed. She looked up at me and smiled. She turned her attention back to her treatment, but now breathing more deeply. A hint of a smile washed across her face as she continued her therapy. I wondered if she was conscious of the same shift that I was sensing.

I turned my attention back to Casandra and watched her. In her new state of relaxation, Casandra reached happily across the table and picked up a set of nesting cups. She calmly entertained herself by carefully stacking and unstacking them. Turning them over, she explored and played with them with contented curiosity. Instinctively, I reached over and joined her in play from the other end of the table. As Marilyn continued her treatment, Casandra joyfully engaged with me, not seeming to even notice the stretching on her leg.

Marilyn looked up, shocked. She appeared bewildered and at the same time relieved to have a window of time to do her therapy with ease. This went on for five or six minutes without a peep. Casandra seemed quite unaware of her leg being stretched, pulled and tapped into therapeutic postures. Marilyn occasionally peered over Casandra's head to catch a glimpse of her patient contentedly playing with her toys. Without saying so, the question hung in the air, "What just happened?" She shook her head slowly as she resumed her treatment.

"She is really liking that toy!" I sensed she was grappling with thoughts trying to make sense of what just happened.

"Yes, by the grace of God, she does seem to be happier, doesn't she?" I said.

"I'm getting a really good long stretch here," Marilyn said with surprise and relief.

Though it was clear that Marilyn did not understand, God's peace and presence of love had shifted things that day. After less than 10 minutes, I left them in a state and relationship they'd never shared before. As I walked out of the door, I glanced over my shoulder to see Casandra playing calmly while Marilyn worked easily with Casandra's leg and ankle. It was a beautiful fresh picture. Smiling, I praised God for his love and mercy.

From that day forward, the school heard no more screaming from their treatment room. Some three months later, I stopped by during their session and asked Marilyn how Casandra was doing.

"She's doing great, no more crying!" she replied emphatically, smiling broadly. "She just lets me work with her. We're making some good progress!"

In that moment, Casandra turned to Marilyn, wrapped her little arms around Marilyn's neck giving her a big hug. Marilyn fully responded in a returned heartfelt embrace. The glow on Marilyn's face reflected her utter enjoyment of Casandra.

"She's like this all the time with me now. We're great buddies! She's turned out to be my favorite kid!"

Marilyn scooped Casandra closer. Casandra snuggled into Marilyn's lap and they sat cheek to cheek, beaming at me.

Looking from Casandra to me, Marilyn said, "It just goes to show you, anyone can change!" as she smiled adoringly at her favorite patient and little friend. I stood in awe at God's grace and mercy, privileged to watch Him do what He does best, create love.

REFLECTIONS:

I have come to understand that God delights in nurturing and deepening loving relationship with Him and reconciling love and peace between His children. God is love. He is not just loving and kind and gentle and good, though all these traits and characteristics surely describe Him. The truth is that He is love. That is His essence, His nature. In praying for people, whether complete healing occurs or not, I always see His signature of a marked increase of love, peace and joy.

As in the case with dear Casandra and Marilyn, relationships are often used, especially through trials and conflicts to help us to learn to surrender our judgments, fears and pain. Relationships are opportunities to come into deeper levels of understanding and acceptance of ourselves and others, to give and receive forgiveness, and to see another afresh through the eyes of God.

The miraculous touch He gave to both of these beloved children of His is so like Him. When I was with the two of them during their therapy sessions, I could almost sense Him weeping over them for the physical and emotional pain they each were suffering. He wanted it to stop because He had compassion for them. He just needed someone who knew how to pray in agreement with His heart to loose the suffering from them and bind God's peace and joy to them. You can too!

The scriptures tell us that what we bind on earth has been bound in heaven and what is loosed on earth is loosed in heaven. God directs us to bind to ourselves the heavenly fruits of the spirit of love, peace, joy, gentleness, kindness, patience, goodness, long-suffering and self-control and to loose away from us all the pain, grief, sorrows and diseases that try to run rampant on the earth. He already paid for it on the cross; now He invites us to stand in our authority and proclaim it on the earth in the precious name of Jesus Christ, Yeshua HaMashiach.

SCRIPTURES:
John 11:35 Jesus (Yeshua) wept. (with compassion) NKJV

Isaiah 63:9 In all their affliction He was afflicted, and the Angel of His Presence saved them; In His love and in His pity He redeemed them and He bore them and carried them all the days of old; NKJV

Matthew 16:19 "And I will give to you the keys of the kingdom of heaven, and whatever you bind on earth will be bound in heaven, and whatever you loose on earth shall be loosed in heaven." NKJV

I Corinthians 13:13 And now abide, faith, hope, love, these three; but the greatest of these is love. NKJV

6

FORLORN TO FREEDOM

I knelt beside her wheelchair and looked up into Lillian's steel blue eyes. Her bony contorted frame lay slumped in her chair. Her vacant, hopeless gaze startled and saddened me. Squatting there beside her, I glanced around the dreary living room of the aging home where she had resided her entire 76 years.

"Hi Miss Lillian. I'm Anita, come to help you with your occupational therapy. How are you today?"

She strained to lift her neck to look toward me. Emitting a soft whimper, she abruptly retreated into her curled posture. I reached up with one hand to massage her neck to release the apparent stiffness. My trained fingertips kneaded her neck for a minute, but I was stunned to find a heavy mound of hardened muscles.

I realized now why she had not looked up as I entered her home. Lillian's rigid neck muscles had nearly riveted her chin to her chest. It was apparent that she was trapped in a confining body tomb. Like a turtle struggling against a heavy, hard shell, Lillian made one final attempt to raise her head, but then collapsed with a groan. We chatted awhile longer while I gathered a beginning understanding of her function and limitations, arranged our next appointment and left for the day.

That afternoon, I returned to the agency office and met with Lillian's physical therapist. A bouncy, enthusiastic blonde approached me carrying Lillian's file.

"Hi I'm Bonnie. How'd it go with Lillian today?"

"Sweet lady but what's going on with her neck?"

"I've been doing hot packs, icing, electrical stimulation, deep massage, even some fascia release for the past 5 months. Unfortunately, I've seen only small gains. She'd do better for a few weeks, show some increased range of motion, then she'd lose it. As a matter of fact, I'm discontinuing treatment."

Later perusing Bonnie's discharge summary, I read her notation, "permanent neck contractures." Head bowed permanently to her chest, she was a frozen memorial of hopelessness, a granite statue displaying the sad representation of a broken spirit.

At our next visit, I completed the initial evaluation which revealed an even more challenging picture. Lillian lived in an upside-down, backwards kind of world. Her massive stroke 15 months earlier left her with perceptual and directional confusion.

"Okay Lillian, let's practice wheeling your chair forward a few feet to the table here and then pull up on the brakes for safety. Do you understand?" I demonstrated several times taking her hands through the movements of propelling forward and braking. "Now you try."

Placing her hands squarely on the wheels, she proceeded to push herself, but unfortunately, she pushed herself backwards. Frustration and confusion washed over her face, as the gap between her chair and the table visibly lengthened. "Okay, okay honey, let's just try it again," I encouraged. More determined now, she placed her hands yet more firmly on the wheels, rocking to and fro for a moment; then she once again propelled herself backwards. Her body slumped deeper in her chair and the disgruntled shake of her head signaled failure.

"That's all right, Lillian. We'll try again later. Take a moment and have a drink of water. Hey, let's try picking up this sock on the floor with your hand-held reacher." I demonstrated with specific instructions numerous times, pointing out visual cues and the sequencing of this simple task. She took the red-handled reacher from me, but turned it end to end. Apparently confused, she rotated and stroked it. Rescuing her from sure defeat, I gently offered her the correct end once again. Repeating her same ritual, she extended the wrong end to the floor, attempting to retrieve the sock with the handle. Frustrated, she threw the reacher down, yelling, "Oh I can never make this d--- thing work!"

Her personal caregivers had been instructed to allow Lillian time to dress herself, as much as possible, in the mornings. Her helper, Anna, told me privately, "She ends up putting both her arms into the sleeves with the back of her shirt covering her chest. No matter how I break it down, I end up just helping her the whole way or she'd never get dressed!"

To complicate matters, I also noted that her family members had come to assume that Lillian was trying to manipulate them. "Wanna try that again?" said her brother Don glibly, lounging on the couch watching TV. Lillian had turned her wheelchair in the wrong direction once again.

"Believe me, she knows exactly what she's doing," Don shared with me privately. "And I ain't goin' there." He had long since decided she was milking him for attention and help. Plans were being considered for giving her antidepressants and pursuing a nursing home placement.

Later that day in our session, Lillian mournfully conveyed through a breathy whisper, "I just want to die. I used to pray for help but no one cares about me. God hates me! I can't stand my family. They don't believe that I get confused!" Her voice erupted into a volcano of rage. "I know they hate me and I hate them! I just want to go home!" The fiery discontent of years of buried bitterness spilled out.

I prayed silently trying to stay clear of the moving lava of her fury, "Oh Father, come and heal her wounds from her past and bring your truth to this family for reconciliation and restoration," I prayed silently.

Shortly thereafter, Barbara, Lillian's daughter-in-law swept into the house. Her scowling demeanor revealed her underlying resentment in her role as caregiver. The subtle yet deliberate clunking of kitchen cabinets echoed through the house as she prepared a sandwich and chicken soup for Lillian. Barbara's false responsibility had bubbled into a frothy environment of resentment and distrust. I knew we needed to talk. Cautiously, I strode into the kitchen, planning to encourage her in her service to her mother-in-law. While the soup simmered, I invited her onto the back porch.

Leaning forward in my chair, I said, "I've noticed you do a lot here Barbara, and it must feel overwhelming. The rehab director told me you've been doing this for a long time." Her arms unfolded from their stoic defensive posture but then she exploded, "She's a witch! She's used me for years. No matter what I do, it's never enough!" Her voice quaked as she laid her forehead in her hands.

I prayed silently for God's wisdom and guidance. Resting my hand on her knee, a new bond was birthed between us. "It's reasonable for you to feel frustrated and overworked. You have a right to your own life. It's understandable to want more rest and to focus on other things you enjoy. We can get more help from the agency and maybe from other family members, as well." Her countenance transformed into stunned disbelief. As she stared across the tree laden backyard, I could almost see her trying to fathom a vision beyond entrapment to this dreaded lifestyle.

After that talk and over the next weeks, I saw a steady change as she took more time for herself. Others in the family stepped up to fill in. I also gave both Don and Barbara a clearer picture of Lillian's actual limitations and needs which seemed to help. Over the next weeks, I sensed a softening in their hearts which appeared to inspire true empathy and compassion toward Lillian.

During this same period, Lillian opened up and shared more of her pain and fears about her disabilities, losses and broken dreams. "I can't do anything for myself and they don't want to help me. Barbara hates me and she's poisoned my son against me. We used to be so close. Why does God hate me? I'm afraid they're just going to put me in one of those old people's homes. I can't see life as being anything but terrible," she anguished.

As she wept, I gently wrapped my arms around Lillian's shoulders and rocked her as a parent would a child in deep distress. I prayed quietly in the Spirit. Through whimpers and tears, she muttered, "God will never forgive me. I've been so angry. I've screamed at Him and my family so many times."

"God never gives up on us, Lillian. Remember that God says in His scriptures, that He will never leave us nor forsake us. He also promises us that He loves us with an everlasting love and that He always forgives us when we ask Him. He says He sends our sins and mistakes as far as the east is from the west." Her breathing slowed and her shoulders relaxed. "He is a God of mercy and kindness and still loves you and desires to heal and bless you," I continued. "We just need to ask Him to forgive us and He is faithful to do that. Would you like to pray with me?"

The peace of God was palpable as we embraced. She leaned toward me as she humbly nodded. With eyes closed, she waited.

"Father God, come and show your daughter your love and kindness. Just ask Him, Lillian, 'Lord, forgive me for the sin of anger, resentment and bitterness toward You and toward my family. I trust You will forgive my mistakes. You promised that You would send my sins as far as the east is from the west, if I ask for forgiveness.' Repeating each phrase, she closed with "I receive your forgiveness today. Thank you Jesus."

I continued, "Jesus, we thank You for healing and delivering her from all her wounds of her body, soul and spirit. You love her and we just thank You for reconciliation and restoration in her life." A tear of joy trickled down my cheek, as I sensed God's mercy for her and watched her receive from a God whom she thought had abandoned her.

In the following week, I noticed some softer and kinder interactions between Lillian and Barbara and her brother, Don. They seemed to be working together with more tenderness and mutual respect. Lillian mentioned that she had a couple of nice talks with Barbara in which she asked Barbara for forgiveness. The whole atmosphere in the home had shifted, which frankly was a welcomed relief.

But that was only the beginning of what God was up to. I'll never forget the day of triumph in God two weeks later when I arrived for our visit. As the screen door slammed behind me, the entire scene morphed into slow motion. I stopped. Was I really seeing this? There sat Lillian, picturesque in her wheelchair, her head and neck held completely upright. As I paused gawking, she slowly turned her head toward me. Looking squarely into Lillian's sparkling eyes and seeing her broad smile, she was fully enjoying my shocked response.

She shared later, "My neck just felt better and better over the weekend. I could just hold it higher and higher. No pain. Jesus healed me!"

Her head held high now, she revealed a new steady gaze at her world, a release from bondage and imprisonment. I stood in awe at this wonderful healing. Lillian and I praised the Lord together for His heart of mercy and kindness.

In the notebook in the home, where caregivers logged progress, it read, "the patient can now lift and turn her head, give eye contact, showing neck flexibility and increased strength." The rigid neck muscles had miraculously released. She now enjoyed newfound freedom and flexibility. That day and for weeks thereafter, Lillian and I praised God's Holy name, for our Lord is truly 'the lifter of our heads'.

Bonnie, her former physical therapist, was astounded by the report that ran rampant through the home health agency. She re-opened her case so she could do deeper treatment with her. Bonnie had been raised as a Christian and this event prompted enthusiastic discussions between us as to God's power to heal today.

"My church taught that miraculous healing was only for the former Bible times," she shared at one point. Her faith soared as she began to reassess many of her patients' potential. She now could view them through a lens of faith and expectation.

By the end of a four month period, we witnessed even deeper restoration for Lillian. She was able to dress and undress herself with only minor assistance. She learned to move from her wheelchair to her bed and lounge chair by herself. Navigating in her wheelchair was a breeze; she loved to grab her reacher to retrieve anything she needed.

"She's doing great, actually," Barbara offered. "She helped me make a PB&J sandwich the other day."

"Pretty impressive," piped up Don.

Antidepressants were dismissed as unnecessary and nursing home placement became irrelevant. But perhaps the most extraordinary change in Lillian was her general state of peace and joy. After her touch from God, she laughed easily. She often looked us in the eyes and smiled broadly. When encouraged, she would share her personal history and speak of God's eternal love for us. By last report, two years later, she's remained in her home.

During one of our final treatment sessions together, a therapist trainee was visiting with me and trying to tap Lillian's elderly wisdom. The earnest student asked, "In your opinion, Miss Lillian, what's the most valuable thing in life?" With humble gratitude, Lillian paused, reflected and then looked deeply at the young woman, "The Lord Jesus Christ died for us and bore our sins on the cross. If we believe in Him, we will live with Him in eternity." Lillian paused, reflected for a brief moment longer and then smiling exclaimed, "You know He's been good to me. He healed me."

REFLECTIONS:

As with Lillian and even her caregiver, Barbara, at the root of suffering can be a need for forgiveness. Bitterness and resentment can literally manifest disease in our bones and our bodies, often leaving us fatigued and devoid of vibrant energy. Bitter-root judgments can cause us to be bound up in our body, soul and spirit, unable to function in the freedom we were intended to enjoy. Liberation into wholeness, joy and peace may involve a need to ask for and receive forgiveness from God and/or to offer and receive forgiveness from others.

When we have been treated unfairly, often we want to wait for the other person to apologize first. We may think that if we apologize for our part, we are letting the other person 'off the hook', so to speak; however it is ourselves that we keep imprisoned. We find our minds and emotions are riddled with anxious, judgmental, shaming, self-pitying, negative thoughts and feelings. When we rise up and take the first step to bring peace into a situation, we find we set ourselves free. We unlock the prison gates and release ourselves and the other person simultaneously which brings freedom and joy to everyone. In this case, Lillian even in her later years was so very blessed to have come to the reality of this powerful truth.

SCRIPTURES:

Proverbs 16:24 Pleasant words are like a honeycomb, sweetness to the soul and health to the bones. NKJV

Matthew 6:14-15 "For if you forgive men their trespasses, your heavenly Father will also forgive you. But if you do not forgive men their trespasses, neither will your Father forgive your trespasses." NKJV

1 John 1:9 If we confess our sins, He is faithful and just to forgive us our sins and to cleanse us from all unrighteousness. NKJV

Psalm 103:12 As far as the east is from the west, so far has He removed our transgressions from us. NKJV

Philippians 4:8 Finally, brethren, whatever things are true, whatever things are noble, whatever things are just, whatever things are pure, whatever things are lovely, whatever things are of good report, if there is any virtue or if there is anything praiseworthy – meditate on these things. NKJV

Psalm 3:3 But You, O Lord, are a shield for me, My glory and the One who lifts up my head. NKJV

7

LIGHT INVADES THE DARKNESS

Christine swept her long brunette hair away from her face to expose gorgeous brown eyes. They reflected wisdom and maturity far beyond her 25 years. I saw later, this came from weathering intense storms, yet learning to stand strong. We sat across from each other in her tiny apartment on our first home visit. I scanned her lovely living room, enjoying the tasteful touches of dried flowers in handspun pottery vases and small exquisitely framed Monet and Renoir prints.

I was struck by Christine's up-beat spirited zeal as she popped up from her chair, saying, "Oops, how silly of me. Can I get you tea or some water? I hope you don't mind but Denise is just finishing her nap. I thought maybe we could talk for a few minutes before she wakes. Okay with you?"

"Oh sure that's fine. And thanks, I would love some water," I responded.

As we settled in, her demeanor sobered as she described the long hours of a tough labor with Denise three years ago, ending in a C-section, only to find her beloved child had been diagnosed with a rare chromosomal abnormality and a profound cognitive handicap.

Christine continued her story as I listened intently. "Then Larry, my boyfriend who is also Denise's daddy, left us. Guess he couldn't take it. He kinda fell apart. He even moved out of state. I'm not even sure where he is…."

Talking about Larry seemed to surface a whole other side of Christine, a place of heartache.

"That's quite a sudden loss right in the middle of so many challenges," I offered.

"You know, I love Denise so much. So grateful for her. She's truly a gift from God. But I gotta admit, at times, it's a lot on my own," she confessed.

A toddler's cry from the bedroom brought us back into the moment. Christine jumped up and headed for the bedroom. She returned smiling, carrying Denise, giving her kisses and hugs as she cradled her in her arms. She brought her to me to introduce us, saying, "Hey Denise, this is our new friend Miss Anita, who came to play with us."

Reaching out to touch her arm, I said, "Hi Denise. So nice to meet you. Did you have a good nap?" It was apparent that Denise was unable to make eye contact or connect in any meaningful way. I knew from the records that she had no language, as yet.

Tenderly, Christine laid Denise on the carpeted floor saying, "She likes to have the freedom to roll around on the rug. I wish she would sit in a chair but she just cries, so I let her stay on the floor mostly."

"That's okay for now. The other therapists and I will help you create special seating that she may like. That's what we're here for. You've been doing real well on your own, so far," I said reassuringly.

I could sense that Christine was having lingering thoughts and feelings from our earlier conversation about Larry. She tucked her folded hands deep into her lap as we watched Denise for a few minutes. Denise maintained a state of perpetual motion, rolling and swaying with her frail legs and knees drawn up to her chin. Though Christine had lovingly dressed her daughter in a colorful floral outfit, pinning her dark auburn hair in fashionable braids with matching clips, Denise still looked quite frenzied and unhappy. As she rolled and rocked on the floor, she continuously jammed one hand and then the other deep in her mouth, sucking, licking and biting on them. Her reddened raw fingers were cracked and scaling from the constant moisture. Periodically, Denise quieted herself long enough to roll onto her side to stare up at a lamp for several minutes. There, mesmerized by the light, she raised a swollen raw hand to shake it in front of her eyes to self-stimulate.

"This is how she is most of the time….." A deep sigh spoke of lost hopes and dreams for her beloved child.

"Do you have other family members in the area to help you?"

"My mom and sister live fairly close and help out some…."

Denise rolled onto a rattle. She picked it up, sucked on it for a moment and then flung it.

"We can't figure out how much she's seeing. The doctors don't seem to know. She just tosses everything."

I prayed as she shared. I was asking Jesus to give me His way of helping this child and mom. Sensing Christine's overwhelm in trying to care for a very needy three year old without much support, I prayed for God's wisdom to ask a key question. Perplexed, I wondered and prayed, *what could I possibly do for Denise and Christine? There are so many needs, Lord…where to start? What would truly bless this mom and her baby?* To this end, I asked,

"Is there anything that you most want help with or have hoped would change as a result of my treatment?"

Christine paused. With apparent hesitation, she looked lovingly at Denise on the floor, and said, "Denise...has done something since birth...that really scares me. Several times a week, for no apparent reason, she just starts kicking, screaming and crying uncontrollably. All my attempts to console her don't work." Choking back tears now, she said, "It goes on for an hour or two."

I must say I was not expecting an even larger issue that seemed to eclipse what I'd already seen. "Oh my, Christine, how upsetting for you. What do you do?"

"I've tried rocking her, singing to her, rubbing her back. Nothing works. I hate to do it, but I end up putting her in her room and just letting her cry it out."

"How does that work?" I asked.

"It takes a long time but finally it stops. She falls asleep from exhaustion, I think." Looking down, she almost whispered, "We've tried everything. My sister, my mom – we've all tried. The doctors don't have any answers. We don't know what else to do...."

She looked solemnly from me to Denise and then asked, "Do you have any ideas?"

Clearly I was stunned by the picture she had just painted. I didn't have a clue. I promised Christine that I would give it some serious thought and consideration. That was code for saying that I would bring it before the Lord in prayer. And I did.

Driving to my afternoon appointments, I couldn't get little Denise off my mind. I knew if the doctors had been consulted, they had ruled out seizures or other physiological issues for which meds might have been given. As I prayed for her, I began to see that these episodes could have a spiritual component. What Christine was describing could be a demonic influence, I thought. I had witnessed children and adults at times tormented by spirits of darkness. Her episodes sounded similar. I knew if these events had a demonic root, it could be playing havoc with Denise's body, soul and spirit. I pondered and prayed. If what I was sensing was true, I knew I was being prepared to pray to break the bondage of these tormenting spirits over this poor child, but I was unsettled by the thought. *How would this happen, in a tiny apartment?* It would have to take God to arrange it.

Two sessions later, I arrived to treat Denise. She was having one of those terrible bouts. As Christine opened the door, visibly shaken she said, "This is what I was telling you about."

Denise lay on the floor, hysterically sobbing, releasing an occasional high-pitched anxious scream, tossing her skinny frame to and fro on the floor in painful writhing. Her contorted face and streaming tears of misery shocked and distressed me. Christine scooped Denise up in an attempt to comfort her but it was apparent that the contact almost made it worse.

"Maybe I should just put her in her room," Christine suggested. "She's been crying a long time."

"Tell you what, let me just go into the room with her and see if there's anything I can do." The Lord was up to something but I didn't know what.

Christine nodded gratefully. I gathered dear Denise in my arms and we headed for the bedroom. Christine placed layers of cushy blankets on the floor. I gently deposited Denise in her comfy haven and sat cross-legged next to her. Thankfully Christine had other things to attend to, so she closed the door behind her. I embarked on trying every calming strategy I knew as a therapist. Gentle patting and firm stroking down her back did nothing for her. I leaned down near her ear and spoke soothingly to her. I sang to her. I tried distracting her with music toys. Nothing fazed her. The screaming and reeling persisted. I prayed, "Lord Jesus, what do you want? What shall I do?"

Very clearly, not audibly but a strong still voice of the Lord within me said, "Take authority." I knew this meant to take authority in His name over tormenting spirits of darkness.

"Thank you, Jesus," I said, grateful to hear His clear direction. Sitting next to Denise, I placed my hand gently on her chest and prayed quietly but firmly. I prayed that by the shed blood of Jesus Christ who died on the cross and who was resurrected, that all demonic tormenting spirits of chaos and destruction must loose themselves from her. Then I called forth the joy, peace, and love of Christ to heal and restore her in the name of Jesus. I felt God's guidance to renounce all demonic strongholds on this child by the authority of Jesus Christ.

As the prayer continued over the next several minutes, Denise's swaying and crying slowed. The palpable peace of God was present in her room. Denise's body stilled. Her hands dropped from her mouth. This child who minutes before was writhing in anguish was now looking up at me with a far calmer countenance.

I gently raised her up to sit facing me. Over the following 10 minutes, I quietly continued to pray healing blessing prayers, speaking scripture blessings over her, like "nothing can separate her from the love of God," and "greater is He (Christ) who was in her than he (satan) who is in the world," and "no weapon formed against her can prosper," and "by Christ's stripes she is healed." Gradually, Denise showed a steady and remarkable shift into complete peace and rest. I watched a gradual transformation into total composure, right before my eyes.

I also noticed that she kept staring over my shoulder and then looking back deeply into my eyes, again over my shoulder and then back to my eyes. She did this over and over. *Was she seeing something or someone?* I wondered. Finally, she did something that thoroughly amazed me. She drew a deep long breath, smiled and leaned fully against my chest. Stunned, but relieved, I returned the embrace. Relaxed with our arms draped around each other, we remained there for many minutes.

At some point, Denise sat up and reached down and picked up a nearby rattle. Looking at it with visible curiosity, she shook it tentatively and smiled. I watched, astonished by her new-found inquisitiveness. This was clearly a breakthrough moment for Denise. I sat spellbound, gawking at her as she examined and shook the rattle. I realized at some point, that I was half-waiting for her usual ritual of licking the rattle and tossing it, but it never happened. I smiled, thanking Jesus for what He had just done.

Though I had somewhat lost track of time, I knew it was getting near the end of the session. I picked up Denise and laid her down in her crib, pointing to a colorful mobile of friendly looking animals hanging over her bed. For the first time in her life, she looked squarely at them and smiled. I shook my head in awe, saying a silent 'Hallelujah' to Jesus.

As I closed her bedroom door behind me, I wondered what I should say to Christine. I didn't sense to try to explain details to Christine about what had transpired. I simply reassured her that I thought Denise had responded well during our time together and that she was resting now. With a grateful handshake, Christine and I said goodbye.

As I left their apartment, I skipped down their cement stairs, taking them two at a time. I was so light on my feet, I felt like I could fly. Climbing into my car, I was grinning with exuberance. It was hard to believe what had just happened and I was there watching it. "Something big just happened, didn't it Lord," I whispered, praising Him as I drove. There was a shift for sure, but how much?

Over the following month as I made visits, Denise appeared calmer overall. She smiled occasionally and seemed to be focusing more. She appeared more connected with people and her environment, even occasionally squeezing and shaking toys. I brought special equipment, showing Denise how to activate special sound and movement toys by pressing their big colorful buttons. Denise seemed to have just awakened. Her doctors and other therapists were no longer questioning her ability to see. It was apparent that she was focusing to play with toys.

Two months passed. I hadn't asked Christine about Denise's episodes. I hadn't seen any, but I knew I could just be missing them. This particular visit, I decided to inquire.

"Christine, I've been meaning to ask, how are those screaming episodes? Are they as frequent?"

I was struck by her response. She paused as if trying to recall something from the distant past.

"Oh, you know…she really hasn't had one of those…for a really long time."

"Oh good. How long would you say?" I asked, stunned but excited. Raising her eyes, trying to recall, she pondered and then said,

"You know, right around the time I talked with you about them, was the last time."

We finally determined that the episodes stopped at the very point when I spent time with Denise in her room, that very day of prayer. Those terrible bouts stopped right then. They were gone, never to return. Denise was a child set free, released from a prison of darkness and torment.

Over the following months, the physical therapist was able to work with Denise on standing and walking. Simultaneously, I started teaching Christine to help Denise feed herself. I still recall the day I arrived for a special visit and walked into the kitchen to find Denise in her highchair. She wore a colorful bib as she proudly picked up and delivered small pieces of fruit to her lips. She looked over at me and smiled as I entered the room. It seemed to me that we were sharing a flashback of our initial private prayer session in her bedroom.

Here was yet another extraordinary moment. Christine beamed. I knew she was thrilled to see Denise reaching goals she had prayed for but thought might never be possible. A new world had opened up for this little one whom God loved and set free from a life of bondage. Our God is an awesome God. His Light dispels the darkness and sets the captives free.

REFLECTIONS:

In this very vivid example with Denise, one can see that even with an innocent, vulnerable babe, powers of darkness can torment and play havoc. Sometimes it has to do with generational issues, trauma, events in the child's life that opened the door, but it clearly required prayers of authority in the name of the Father, His Son, Jesus and Holy Spirit. If we do not know there is victory through Jesus Christ, we can be unnecessarily tormented.

Sometimes in our own lives, persisting anxiety, depression or a nagging physical condition can require a spiritual cure. The worldly answer is to find the right therapist, the right drug, the right stress management program, or the newest alternative remedy. Though these approaches may be helpful to relieve symptoms, these strategies may only give temporary relief if there is a demonic component. The ultimate breakthrough into permanent freedom may involve calling upon God who is the comforter, healer and deliverer.

Many times we struggle with whether our challenges have to do with our own dark sides, unresolved fears, or pressures from the world. There is, however, yet another component to consider: that of a spiritual attack. It is, of course, always prudent to examine in depth what we are feeling or experiencing. Seeking wisdom about fears and conflicts is always vital. We don't want to be trying to cast out demons for what could be psychological or emotional issues, which call for a change in our own thoughts or behavior. Even if this be the case, if we bring it to God, He can give direction to bring wholeness.

However we do not want to dismiss the aspect that within these very real struggles of the heart and mind, the powers of darkness may be taking advantage of the conflict within us. With all the examination of the self in the world today, it is not uncommon to deny or have difficulty discerning the demonic within a situation. It is real and must be handled with clarity and focus. Many times, we open the door for Satan to enter into situations by remaining in denial of the reality of the powers of darkness.

But in all of this, we can take heart in the knowledge that as the scripture reminds us 'greater is He who is within you, than he that is in the world.' We are further instructed that the demonic must flee when renounced in the name of Jesus Christ, Son of God, who came in the flesh. We have been given the keys to the kingdom of heaven and authority over the demonic through the blood covenant of Christ Jesus. The demonic has no real power and certainly no more power than we give it.

SCRIPTURES:

Ephesians 6: 12-13 For we do not wrestle against flesh and blood, but against principalities, against powers, against the rulers of the darkness of this age, against spiritual hosts of wickedness in the heavenly places. Therefore take up the whole armor of God, that you may be able to withstand in the evil day, and having done all, to stand. NKJV

I John 4:4 You are of God, little children, and have overcome them, because He who is in you is greater than he who is in the world. NKJV

Isaiah 54:17 "No weapon formed against you shall prosper, and every tongue which rises against you in judgment, You shall condemn. This is the heritage of the servants of the LORD, and their righteousness is from Me," says the LORD. NKJ

Isaiah 53: 4-5 Surely He has borne our griefs and carried our sorrows; Yet we esteemed Him stricken, smitten by God, and afflicted. But He was wounded for our transgressions, He was bruised for our iniquities; the chastisement for our peace was upon Him, And by His stripes we are healed. NKJV

Romans 8: 38-89 For I am persuaded that neither death nor life, nor angels nor principalities nor powers, nor things present nor things to come, nor height nor depth, nor any other created thing, shall be able to separate us from the love of God which is in Christ Jesus our Lord. NKJV

1 John 4: 3-4 and every spirit that does not confess that Jesus Christ has come in the flesh is not of God. And this is the spirit of the Antichrist, which you have heard was coming, and is now already in the world. You are of God, little children, and have overcome them, because He who is in you is greater than he who is in the world. NKJV

8

LOVE CONFOUNDS CANCER

Betty and Ruth were buddies, roommates at Brentwood Assisted Living for 5 years. They were dear friends sharing the ups and downs of aging and giving selfless support. They also knew how to enjoy a good laugh. With that foundation they were more prepared than most for what was coming.

Ruth sat in her lounge chair as she teased Betty. Ruth's short cropped silver hair framed a warm friendly face. She sported a very serious expression as she began explaining her story.

"I'm telling you Anita, venturing into the bathroom some days is like going on a jungle safari plowing through the rows of Betty's stockings," Ruth finished with a rosy-cheeked smile.

Betty's shoulders rocked as she giggled, sitting there in her wheelchair, taking her guff like a seasoned veteran. Ruth and Betty enjoyed telling stories on each other, but it was all in good fun. As I listened and smiled, you could almost see the wheels turning in Betty's head, preparing her comeback.

"Well, Ruth honey, I have to do something in the middle of the night, when you doze off early and rock the west wing with your snoring…good thing that's just when you're really over-tired and exhausted," she added quickly checking that her teasing hadn't hurt her friend's feelings. Ruth smiled and nodded her head, not the least bit offended.

"Yeah, I guess I can give a chainsaw a run for its money on those nights, I hear tell." I chuckled, rather privileged to have them invite me into their world.

I was assigned as Betty's occupational therapist to help her with her Muscular Dystrophy. Although she was still quite independent from her wheelchair, my job was to attend to any changing needs she might have. And recently, Betty's life had taken a huge turn; her risks and challenges rose dramatically overnight, because Betty just received a diagnosis of pancreatic cancer.

That came as a real blow to both her and Ruth, especially in light of the fact that it was April; early June was the anniversary of Betty's son's death 6 years earlier. Though it can be normal to grieve the loss of a loved one on the anniversary of their death as memories surface -- with Betty it was different. Historically, each year in June since her son's tragic motorcycle accident, she mourned to the point of a near psychotic break. The staff was already preparing to support her through this year's deep tribulation when they discovered the pancreatic cancer.

Needing to check in on these more serious matters, I switched gears from the playful humor. "So how have you been feeling, Betty?"

She paused, reflecting for a moment. I studied her lovely features as she thought. Though her face had become pale and shallow, revealing even more distinctly her high cheek bones, she was still stunning at 57 years.

"I'm trying to keep hopeful about the cancer. They started me on chemotherapy treatments. I feel nauseated and weak a lot. They're changing my diet. Giving me more veggie and fruit smoothies, but I don't have much of an appetite. I just feel so darn weak and sick all the time. Sleep a lot. Frankly, I'm pretty scared. Overwhelmed." She looked down, tears pooling in her eyes.

"Oh Betty, so sorry it's been so hard," I sympathized. I frankly couldn't help but think to myself, *Lord, how much can one person take?*

She mumbled, "Thanks." as she tucked her shawl tighter around her shoulders.

"Do you need an extra blanket honey?" Ruth asked. "Seems she gets cold real easy now."

I grabbed a crocheted afghan from the foot of her bed and laid it across her lap as we continued. "Are the extra visits with the nurse and personal aide helping?" I asked gently. "I know you're used to doing things for yourself. I was just hoping you'd conserve energy and get more rest with more help."

"I know. Ruth keeps telling me that. Those new gals are nice, but I like things done my way, ya know." She shot a grin to her faithful friend. "Ruth and I have been reading the Bible more together. Sometimes Ruthie reads while I just relax."

"Can I get you a glass of water, honey? More water seems to help her," Ruth offered.

I watched Ruth wince as she pressed her gnarled hands against the arms of her chair to rise to fetch the water. Struggling with painful arthritis herself, she still was eager to bring comfort to her friend. I knew Ruth and I both longed for Betty to get a touch of healing from the Lord. Betty was fortunate to have a faithful praying friend like Ruth to walk her through this difficult time, and Betty knew it. Betty's son, Danny had been about the only family she had left, before the accident.

Betty and I talked a while longer about ways she could pace herself. She seemed to hear in a fresh way that she needed to give herself permission to let others do more for her. I left that day seeking God in prayer to bring Betty healing, comfort and a deeper capacity to receive.

At our next session, the following week, I arrived to find Betty clutching and rubbing her right shoulder.

"It hurts all the time, Anita. I haven't slept all weekend," Betty whimpered.

Ruth's pale sleep-deprived face witnessed to the disruption of the rhythm in their shared studio. Ruth nervously reached across the bedside table, fumbling for a tube of muscular cream saying, "Can you put some of this on her? It doesn't seem to do much, but it's all we have," she asked.

"Yes, of course," I responded.

As I washed my hands, I prayed silently, seeking the Lord for His direction. As I unscrewed the cap and squeezed a dab of the cream into my palm, I was reminded that the Lord Himself is a balm of healing love. I knew this was a prompting from the Holy Spirit to trust and agree with God for bigger things than just temporary relief.

"You know ladies," I said, "I can apply this lotion, but let's remember that our Lord Jesus Christ himself is a balm of love and grace that goes to the root of our need for healing. How about we agree to apply the Lord's balm of healing goodness? It will go deeper to heal all He wants to touch today."

As I rubbed the cream into her shoulder, I prayed aloud as we agreed for God's deep touch. As we continued to pray, something remarkable started to occur. It doesn't happen often, but there it was. I felt a manifestation of heat flowing. My hand and her shoulder were getting increasingly warm.

"Wow, what's that?" Betty exclaimed in response to the feeling of heat. Her eyes wide now, she looked over at Ruth saying, "My shoulder's really hot."

Ruth sat up in her chair, watching her friend closely. She asked, "Are you okay? That cream usually makes your shoulder feel cold."

"It's okay," I explained, "sometimes the Holy Spirit gives a manifestation of God's healing power and presence with warmth."

"It's hot. Oh, feels good. So-o-o good. Feel such peace," Betty's voice softened. Her eyelids fluttered a bit before she closed them, as she took a long deep breath and eased more deeply into her wheelchair.

"Yes, just relax and receive the warmth of God's healing touch for you, Betty," I encouraged as I continued to simply maintain my hand gently on her shoulder. The three of us just sat there, thanking God for what He was doing. We were silent in this sweet atmosphere of God's love and holy presence.

As we waited, I discerned God wanting to move in a still greater way for Betty. After several minutes, I felt prompted to pray in boldness for the Lord not only to take away her shoulder pain but to heal the cancer completely. Still further, I prayed that Betty would be protected from all side effects of the chemotherapy. That was a strong and bold prayer but I perceived I was praying the heart and will of the Father for her. As I spoke this out in faith, we all agreed and thanked the Lord for doing all He wanted to do.

Two weeks passed before I was over at the Brentwood facility again. As I was heading down their hall, Ruth motioned to me from her doorway; enthusiastically she entreated me to come quickly. Entering the room, Betty erupted,

"From the moment we prayed..." she said beaming.

"Yeah! That same day," continued Ruth.

"My shoulder's been pain-free," finished Betty.

Like two school girls, stumbling over each other trying to tell the story, their giggles and squeals were contagious. Their happy demeanors reflected what God had done. I suspected they'd told this story many times, to many people.

I was taken aback. Although, I'd had a strong sense that the Lord had deeply touched Betty when we prayed, hearing about this dramatic impact was astounding. We thanked Jesus together. God's sweet presence filled the room all over again as we shared. As we were still marveling at God's goodness, Betty continued,

"You know what else?"

I shook my head, not knowing if I could take much more.

"Since that day, I've felt better and stronger than I have in months, right Ruthie?"

Ruth said, "Oh yes, you've been doin' great!"

"And the best part?" Betty beamed, "no side effects from the chemotherapy!"

Ruth sat nodding and smiling saying, "It's wonderful. She's eatin' double portions. Back to her old self again." Betty and Ruth chuckled together. "No, but seriously," Ruth continued, "she's eating great and she has lots of energy." With excitement and gratitude, the three of us just thanked God for His kindness and mercy for touching Betty so deeply.

Two months passed. Betty thankfully made it through the anniversary of Danny's death riding the wave of her feelings with more balance. She talked through special memories about her boy with Ruthie and some of the staff. This was quite a breakthrough for Betty, reflecting the gift of God's peace of mind to her soul.

When I arrived for one of our last appointments in September, there was a buzz in the air again. Ruth and Betty were in a mode of excitement and delight.

"I got a phone call and next week, someone from the hospital wants to make a visit and do an interview with me," Betty bubbled. "Their tests are showing no more cancer! And the woman said they want to do a profile on me, 'cause of how well the chemotherapy worked. I know they're real surprised how I got through all that chemo with no side effects."

Ruth piped in, "But we know how she made it through so well."

"Yes and I'm gonna tell 'em. I'm giving my Lord the honor and glory for the victory of my recovery," exclaimed Betty.

"And I'll be right here to be a witness. God's the hero in this one," Ruth exclaimed, so happy to have her friend back and in good health. They both had been strengthened in their faith through this journey with God who moved so powerfully and lovingly.

"Of course, I'm real grateful for all the medical help," Betty added. "I just want them to hear how prayer changed everything in one day. Hope my story encourages them to pray even more for their patients."

REFLECTIONS:

Betty's and Ruth's passionate testimonies encouraged me to more fervently press into God to seek His guidance as to how and when to pray for my patients. We in the medical field as well as family members all need to be encouraged to pray and partner with God in His healing process. Because we are made in His image, our very unction to see the sick healed and comforted comes from Him. So if we ask God for His strategy or His way to pray, He loves to bless us with specific insight and understanding. What better colleague or partner could we have than our Creator who knows how to heal us?

I will be forever grateful to Betty and Ruth for their spontaneous authentic walk with God and one another. Their shared loving humor borne out of caring relationship helped them through trials. I watched them agree in prayer around important issues that inspired great hope in their great need. Sharing the scriptures by reading together brought the power and wisdom of God into their midst which ushered in God's presence for breakthrough. I was personally transformed as God moved in such a profound way in their rich shared life.

SCRIPTURES:

Proverbs 17:22 A merry heart does good, like medicine, but a broken spirit dries the bones. NKJV

1 John 4:7-8 Beloved, let us love one another, for love is of God; and everyone who loves is born of God and knows God. He who does not love does not know God, for God is love. NKJV

James 5:16 Confess your trespasses to one another, and pray for one another, that you may be healed. The effective, fervent prayer of a righteous man avails much. NKJV

Isaiah 40:8 The grass withers, the flower fades, But the word of our God stands forever. NKJV

2 Timothy 1: 8-9 Therefore do not be ashamed of the testimony of the Lord, nor of me His prisoner, but share with me in the sufferings for the gospel according to the power of God, who has saved us and called us with a holy calling, not according to our works, but according to His own purpose and grace which was given to us in Christ Jesus before time began. NKJV

9

FLOURISHING IN INFANCY

Ten-month-old Daniel was dying a slow death. His family and I exchanged anguished glances as we sat fixated on this scrawny babe during our first visits. Grandma Becca, Aunt Carol and Daniel's mom, Angie were in a tailspin trying hard to reverse the downward spiral of 'failure to thrive' which he'd been labeled. His reflux disorder was triggering Daniel's food back up his esophagus; his wasting frame testified to his struggles. This situation would have overwhelmed even the most veteran moms, but for Angie at 18 years, everything was magnified. Sam, her wayward boyfriend, Daniel's daddy, was more attached to drinking with his buddies than he was to his baby or Angie. He was just a kid himself.

Becca cupped my arm and steered me gently but firmly to a far corner of the room. "Angie had another one of them panic attacks last night," whispered Becca. She worried for her grandson and her daughter.

"I've tried everything I know," moaned young Angie, her eyes darting toward Becca. Angie searched her mother's face to see if Becca could recall something, anything they may have missed that could help her son. Becca sat on the couch, shoulders slouched. Her disheveled appearance testified to a life consumed with keeping an infant alive.

"Ain't ever seen anything like it. I raised 5 kids and helped with my all my sister's kids. We never seen nothing like this. He's such a cutie but he just can't keep his food down." Her gaze turned to her other daughter, Carol. "Your kids always ate good, right?"

"Yeah, but you just gotta burp 'em more. He's probably just got gas!" offered Carol. "I told you Angie, if you'd just…."

Angie swooped up her coffee cup and escaped abruptly to the kitchen while Becca shushed Carol. Carol completed with a sing-songy, "Well, okay then." The screen door shut behind her with a dull thud, as Carol retreated to the front porch swing. Protected from the line of fire, she remained within earshot. Everyone's nerves were frayed. They were desperate for answers.

Angie returned. She carefully nestled baby Daniel in her arms, positioning spit up towels under his chin and over his chest. Exhausted from repeated tries, she was again bracing herself for one more attempt to keep his formula down. He needed to gain weight; everything depended on it.

The nearly jaundiced baby looked hungrily at his bottle. All natural reflexes were operating as his little hands and arms undulated at the sight and smell of his precious milk. I could tell he was famished, but eating had become a battleground. I looked on as this frightened mom angled the infamous bottle toward her son's lips. Daniel's tongue and lips gingerly tested the edge of the nipple before latching on.

"Yes," I said under my breath with hope and anticipation.

"Some is going in…." Angie said excitedly.

Becca blurted out, "Oh no-o-o!" Gasps of disappointment erupted from all three of us as we watched Daniel spew his formula up out of his mouth, once again. The terror in his eyes seemed to implore, "Make it stop!" On cue, his formula came surging up his throat and out his little nose. Bewilderment and sadness hung in the room.

"Can I try?" I offered cautiously. I waited from my cross-legged position on the floor as she cuddled Daniel. "I know you must be so tired. I've got a couple of ideas."

I knew she didn't fully trust any of the medical team, particularly because so much of what had been tried still hadn't kept his food down. A wall of suspicion had risen; it was disrupting a bond of trust which ideally would be there by now in such a dire situation. I couldn't really blame her. A newborn that is not thriving is every parent's worst nightmare.

Her hands shook nervously as she lifted Daniel's tiny body to me. I caught a glimpse of veiled hope in her eyes; she so longed for relief for her beloved child. Instructing a family with a baby in such a critical situation was never easy. I prayed silently that the Lord would give me creative insight and wisdom.

I scrambled from the carpet to find a comfortable position on the far end of the couch, receiving Daniel to my chest. Drawing on every therapeutic strategy I knew, I cradled the babe in my arms. Using pillows around him for support, I angled his tiny head, neck and shoulders to create the best posture for swallowing. I tapped his little shoulders and arms forward to relax them. I knew his tight neck and shoulders were part of the larger issue defeating our valiant efforts. I tried the best feeding approaches, but that day and for so many to follow, his tight muscle patterns persisted and only small amounts of formula stayed down.

A few weeks later at a subsequent session, Angie said, "Look! I tapped his shoulders, I stretched him with those special exercises you gave me but then watch." As she placed sweet Daniel on his side, supported with cushions, his little shoulders recoiled like a tight slingshot.

He was now going on 11 months and his rigid little body stood in the way of his rolling over or sitting on his own. Over many sessions, the family tried repeatedly to relax Daniel's rigid, tiny arms and shoulders. Daniel couldn't hold a toy or his bottle with his two hands together; the tightness added to the refluxing of his food. He was looking paler and sicker as the weeks went by.

To complicate matters, Angie refused to give Daniel the medications that the clinic prescribed for his reflux disorder. "I'm not giving him that stuff," insisted Angie. "Makes him cry and gives him gas! That's all we need with everything else!" Under pressure from the team, she occasionally administered a small amount. But we knew, even she knew, that without regularity, the drug was useless. Consistency was needed to create a cumulative effect in the body. The doctors were considering readmitting him to the hospital. The previous hospital stays provided some periods of tube feeding to stabilize him, but on his own, his reflux was still dominating.

"What can we do, Anita?" whimpered Angie. "Mama and me prayed last night. Even Carol came over. We asked God to help Danny. We don't know what to do." Angie's desperation had finally broken through the barrier of her distrust. She was genuinely asking for help.

In the quiet sanctuary of my home the night before, I had prayed as I had so often for this babe and his family. Who knows the timing of the miraculous? One day we will understand it. But on this day, I felt there was a strategic moment in the spiritual realm that might allow me to stand with them in prayer for breakthrough.

I knew I was taking a chance to speak so boldly but with her sharing about her family praying the night before, I took the leap. "How about we join in prayer together and then see how he'll do today?" I prayed silently for a softening of her heart to the idea.

"Okay," she half muttered but it was the sweetest one word I believe I had ever heard from her lips. On cue, she turned toward the kitchen to invite Becca and Carol to join us. I could see she was eager to receive from God.

I knew so much depended on the four of us agreeing in prayer. The multiplication effect in prayer is so powerful. I'd seen it so many times. We formed a circle around Daniel. We were about to push back powers of darkness that were trying to bring death and destruction. Calling on the light and love of God, we were erecting a mighty fortress of faith. Reaching out to take the hands of Angie and Carol triggered a ripple effect and soon we had formed a circle of clasped hands with Daniel in the center, gazing up at us.

We each took a turn praying for Jesus to heal and deliver Daniel. We thanked and praised God for moving and restoring sweet Daniel to health and wholeness. Upon closing, we nodded to one another with reassuring smiles like a beleaguered army mustering up hope for a final victory in a long fought battle. Maybe, just maybe this time it will be different, I half hoped and half prayed.

Angie snuggled Daniel in her arms with pillows propped. But this time, there was potent expectation in the air. Peace fell. It was so palpable that Angie herself let out a long exhale. Daniel gazed around, cooing sweetly. I could feel God's peace. Optimism was tangible. Daniel's little lips latched tentatively around the bottle's nipple. He visibly relaxed with an audible sigh. That expelling breath from that babe ushered in a new era.

In awe, we watched as one of his little hands reached forward and touched the edge of the bottle. That was a breakthrough in itself. We had never seen his tight shoulder muscle relax enough to reach and touch the bottle. He latched onto the nipple with his lips. He sucked several times. He paused, then sucked again, stopped and held his grip on the nipple with his tongue. His eyes blinked and looked up at his mama. We glanced around at one another; clearly something was different. He sucked again, then stopped and gazed at us. He didn't look stressed or fearful. As a matter of fact, I thought I perceived a little twinkle in his eye and a tiny flash of a smile. I held my breath, afraid to break the silence or in any way alter the atmosphere. No one spoke. Again he sucked and paused – sucked and paused – content and steady in his sucking and swallowing.

Angie signaled to us with raised eyebrows to take note of the measurement on the bottle showing, he had consumed one entire ounce. That one ounce moved to one and a half, then amazingly to two ounces. We were mesmerized by the descending level of formula. We sat together exchanging solemn but excited glances. No one dared speak. An occasional cautious smile swept over one face after another. My inner prayer of thanks and praise continued throughout, as hopeful gasps turned into suppressed squeals from Becca and Carol. Cautious giggles erupted into unrestrained laughter when we saw that Daniel had consumed close to four full ounces.

We had just witnessed a miracle and we knew it, a truly glorious breakthrough. The Lord was healing Daniel before our very eyes. Angie held up the near empty bottle in a proclamation of victory. Whoops and yelps from us led to hugs and praising a faithful God.

Over the next three weeks of treatment, Daniel kept down 80 to 90 per cent of his formula. His pallid, drawn face morphed into a pudgy, rosy demeanor. His arms and legs filled out and firmed up. His clear eyes and frequent smiles evidenced his newfound health and contentment. We were thrilled!

The medical clinic checkups reported regular and rapid weight gain. Within a month, Daniel was taken off 'failure to thrive' status. The clinic staff was aware of mom's reluctance to give Daniel the medication and assumed she'd changed her mind. However, the family knew the true remedy. What brought Daniel into wholeness was God wrapping His healing arms of mercy around him.

At one of our final visits, Angie rushed through the front door, Daniel in one arm clutching the clinic report in the other. "His muscles are all okay! Just like you said, Anita, they thought his shoulders and neck weren't tight anymore." It was so wonderful to join with the family to gaze spellbound at our new little gymnast who couldn't be stopped. To our delight, Daniel progressed from rolling to sitting on his own.

Finally the big day arrived! I watched as Angie coaxed Daniel to take his first steps into her arms. Our cheers spoke to our gratitude to a God who loves His children. Carol and Becca grabbed each other in an enthusiastic hug, praising a God of goodness and might. It had been a long treacherous journey. I thanked God for healing Daniel and restoring hope and faith to an entire family.

REFLECTIONS:

Years after this astounding healing event of this infant, I revisited his neighborhood in hopes of finding him and his family. By memory, I drove straight to their home, climbed out of my car and began to stroll down his street in nostalgic wonder. I gazed at the old Victorian style home I'd entered so many times. Standing mesmerized, I smiled recalling the trek up that tall flight of cement steps to their door. Then I imagined being welcomed in, sitting on the floor with mom, baby and grandma, praying and seeing the Lord's hand of love restore another child's life.

As I pondered and mused, a nearby neighbor while watering her flowers waved a friendly hello. As we reacquainted ourselves, she explained that though the family had moved, she was still in touch with them. She had the opportunity to volunteer as an aide in Daniel's elementary classroom for two years. As we reflected together she shared, "Oh that was nothing short of a miracle of God, the way that little boy turned around. Just started eating. Everyone knew it."

She went on to say that Daniel grew to be an especially tender-hearted boy and that he still holds a special place in her heart. She praised the Lord for His goodness and kindness for what He'd done for that family. I was grateful to the Lord for allowing me to cross paths with that neighbor to learn how that sweet baby had matured after his challenging early beginnings.

"Jesus loves the little children, all the children of the world," so the song goes. And we are His children. The manifestation of God's love for children is a blessing to behold. Children are so open and have no barriers to receiving God's goodness and healing mercies. We are called to become like children. 'In order to enter the kingdom of heaven, you must become like little children,' the scriptures tell us. We are encouraged to become open and receptive, trusting in the possibility of supernatural grace and healing. Father God reaches out to us wanting to give to us. He wants us to receive His touch just as Daniel in his innocence was able to receive.

SCRIPTURES:

Hebrews 11:1 Now faith is the substance of things hoped for, the evidence of things not seen. NKJV

Matthew 18: 2-4 Then Jesus called a little child to Him, set him in the midst of them and said, "Assuredly, I say to you unless you are converted and become as little children, you will by no means enter the kingdom of heaven. Therefore whoever humbles himself as this little child is the greatest in the kingdom of heaven." NKJV

Matthew 18: 19-21 "Again I say to you if two of you agree on earth concerning anything that they ask, it will be done for them by My Father in heaven. For where two or three are gathered together in My name, I am there in the midst of them." NKJV

10

FROM DEATH'S DOOR

My eyes were immediately drawn to Louisa's emaciated, scaling legs and bleeding, raw calves. A slight shudder arose in my belly. Even after years as a therapist and raising four boys who got dozens of cuts, the sight of torn, bloody skin still brought an empathetic pang in my gut. Louisa and I exchanged frowns sharing an unspoken wish for relief. Her daughter Virginia, looked on, not saying a word.

"Come touch my back, honey." Louisa rolled up her flowered shirt and leaned forward slowly, allowing me to examine a bulging area on her right low back. I was jolted. I was staring at a tumor the size of a large grapefruit. From her records, I knew it was cancerous. As I gently touched the mass, she jerked away. I scolded myself inside wishing I had not caused more pain, even for a moment.

Eighty-one years of hopeful smiles left distinctive creases on Louisa's elegant, black face. But I sensed these recent months of pain were sculpting deeper routes on her worried brow. Louisa sat on her porch swing cocooned in pillows which Virginia had gathered to offer a measure of comfort. Louisa's weakening legs could no longer propel her on the swing, a statement of her once active life slowing to a standstill.

"Can't find a way to sit or lay to get comfortable. I can't sleep much either," she moaned. Dark circles surrounded her pained eyes. She searched my face for hope. Her silver streaked, black hair, matted on one side reflected her on-going night time struggles.

Virginia stood near us like a rear guard, silent but steady, armored for the battle that had been waging against her mother. She fluffed her mom's pillows and brushed a wisp of hair from her brow before stepping back into battalion position.

"What do you think of these?" Louisa jutted her left forearm toward me to reveal numerous bulging hard masses. Seven jaw-breaker size purplish-blue tumors protruded from her frail appendage, evidencing further her diagnosis of terminal cancer.

"These scare me. What do you think?" Thankfully not waiting for my answer, she continued.

"I'm just exhausted. My back hurts so bad. I just can't sleep at night. My stomach gets real upset. Can't keep anything down."

Virginia, who'd come down from Grand Rapids to care for her mother, tried to quell her mother's rising distress. "Oh mama, now don't be gettin' yourself upset again. Maybe this nice lady can help us figure out how you can feel more comfortable."

Virginia invited me out of the mobile home and onto the gravel driveway for a private talk. Tears welled as she spoke. "Hospice has been called. Surgery and chemo would be too hard on her. The doc says she's got two months at the most."

She looked away. The dam broke. I reached out to hold this dear daughter. She welcomed my arms. Two meeting hearts to better carry the weight of such a tragic burden. Arm in arm, we strolled further away from the house to allow Virginia time to release emotions and eventually regain composure. As we walked, I noted the brown wasting grass and withering flowers peeking through overgrown weeds. I grieved inside with her for the looming loss of her beloved mother.

Leaving the mobile home that day I wondered, *why have I been called in on this case?* Usually, I was referred patients to help them return to a full life, not exit it. This situation called for just helping her feel more comfortable, I decided. *I guess I can adapt special pads and pillows for her last few weeks.* I was a bit in shock. I needed time to pray.

Three days passed before I drove down their long, winding driveway again. I was in turmoil. My heart raced, wondering if she had even made it through the previous nights. *Surely the office would have informed me if... but sometimes they get so busy down there.* I reassured myself that the doctors had given her a month or two to live. As I pulled to a stop, I braced myself. I didn't want to say goodbye to such a sweet, elder woman nor comfort a grieving daughter who clearly was not ready to see her mama go.

I gingerly managed the deteriorating front steps of their mobile home. A gust of wind flapped a torn corner of the porch screen. I held my breath and knocked on the door. Virginia's warm yet somber face welcomed me.

"Come on in. We're ready for you." I blew out an audible breath. The door's squeak covered my involuntary expression of relief. "Mom's waitin' on you." She directed me across rag rugs and decaying tiles, down a narrow hallway. Family photos hung askew along the length of the worn interior paneling.

At her bedroom doorway, I caught a glimpse of the gold-edged pages of Louisa's well-worn Bible on her bedside stand. A laced, fringed lampshade shed subtle rays into her dimly lit space. Mounds of quilts encircled her for her long, difficult nights. Louisa's strong, ebony face greeted me. I sensed her brave smile reflected years of drawing on deep reserves of faith in God.

"I just hurt, honey! I barely slept last night. But I know the good Lord loves me!" A suppressed tear defied my strong professional demeanor. A guarded sigh slipped from my lips. Virginia's hacking cough announced her entrance from behind me as she handed her mom a glass of water. "She smokes too much," mama worried out loud. This mother and child feared and dreaded for each other.

"You know Jesus has always watched over me. He's good, so good, all the time." Louisa spoke valiantly from her deep well of trust in Him.

This so heartened me. Her candor about her beliefs overrode my normal caution to offer spoken prayer.

"Would you like to pray together?" They answered simultaneously in stereophonic sound. "Yes, yes please!"

And pray we did, each time I came. We prayed for comfort, peace and strength at first. Virginia assisted me in fashioning more sophisticated positioning foam and cushions. Over the ensuing three weeks, Louisa and I embarked on light strengthening activities from her bed. Several sessions allowed Louisa time to recollect her life, both victories and challenges. We would close each session in fervent prayer. I noted her condition was not improving, yet not worsening. She did seem to be resting better at night.

A weekend had passed since our last session. As I approached the mobile home, I could see Louisa on the porch swing beaming. Virginia swung open the screen door, obviously eager for my arrival. As I climbed the porch steps, Louisa squealed, "Look, look Anita!" extending her left arm to me. "They're all gone! Sunday morning I woke up and they weren't there!" Virginia watched my face, intent to see my reaction.

I couldn't believe my eyes. Louisa's left arm was now as smooth and normal as her right. I grabbed her wrist and stroked it. I lifted her arm to examine it further. Everything was normal, no more masses, no more discoloration. My head ratcheted between Virginia and Louisa. I looked. I stroked. I was speechless. And then I yelled, "Glory to God!" I laughed. I cried, raising my hand in spontaneous thanks to God.

"I just woke up Sunday morning and they were gone, right Virginia?"

With the first toothy smile I had ever seen on Virginia, she exclaimed, "Yes, Yes! Mama was yelling 'Ginny, get in here. Look at this!' I came runnin' in, not knowing what happened, but there she was, standin' in front of her mirror, touching her arm, saying 'O-o-oh, thank you Jesus. O-o-oh, thank you Jesus!' We praised him for a long time, didn't we mama? Yes we did. Woo-hoo! Our God is good!" She shuffled a little circle jig right there on the porch.

"And look at my legs!" Louisa pulled up her long dress above her knees unveiling smooth healed skin. Her raw, scaling calves were now healthy and clear. Surprised, I stepped right back into Virginia. She held me in a kind of steadying cuddle. She and I shared a long knowing look as I gazed across my shoulder at her. "Yes, yes," she exclaimed. "They canceled Hospice yesterday after the nurse came out. They said they'd just wait and see--yep, just wait and see!" She looked back to her mom with a big grin.

Louisa blurted out, "I told the nurse. I knew God was healin' me. Well you know, she just kinda shook her head. I knew she was real surprised, 'cause she's the same one who examined me before. This time she looked at my arm four or five times, real thorough. Love to hear what she told her family about her day at work. She was awful glad when I told her I was getting my appetite back and eating more and keeping it all down. She was real happy about that, wasn't she, Ginny?"

Virginia nodded and smiled. Her armor appeared to be resting a bit more comfortably on her faithful shoulders. She was starting to see that her Captain General God was leading the ranks closer to victory. We stood in awe and allegiance to a faithful God. Grasping one another's grateful hands, we prayed with a whole new level of expectation for a complete healing of gallbladder cancer.

At subsequent sessions, Louisa starting poking at the bulging tumor on her back, saying, "It just ain't that tender anymore." A few weeks later, she said, "I'm sleeping better." In a month, she said, "The doctor said it wasn't gettin' any bigger, but Ginny and I think it's even smaller."

Four months from my first session, I knocked at her door and was greeted by Louisa herself. Virginia had gone home because she just wasn't needed anymore. Louisa made a sandwich for herself and placed it between us on the couch. She pulled up the back of her shirt just as we had on that first day together. I swept my hand across her back and felt nothing but smooth normal skin. Perfect back formation had replaced the swollen enlarged tumor. I could even feel her lower rib bones which had been masked by the persistent inflamed tissue.

With a full, cheeky grin, Louisa arose from her chair. She fixed me a cup of tea and returned carrying a large envelope. "I got this in the mail two days ago. I was gonna call you, but I just had to see your face when you read it."

I took some sheets from her that she pulled from the envelope. My eyes followed item by item down a complete lab and MRI report. The far right column read NORMAL from top to bottom. Her gallbladder and every other organ were free of all cancer. All systems were functioning normally. Stunned, but smiling back at her, I could only utter, "Wow, what did the doctor say?"

"Well, he said, 'Louisa, you're healthier now than you were 10 years ago!' But I just told him, 'My Jesus, He snatched me from death's door!' Yes, He did Nita; my Jesus snatched me from death's door."

That was my last visit with Louisa. I kept in touch with Louisa and Virginia by phone for many months. Virginia told me Louisa's church broke out in a revival seeing her miraculous recovery, which built faith for many other healings to follow. When traveling in the Wisconsin area some years later, her next door neighbor told me that Louisa lived another four healthy years after her healing. She passed into the arms of her beloved Jesus, a natural death at 85. Her sweet Jesus greeted her with open arms at heaven's gate at His perfectly appointed time.

REFLECTIONS:

Louisa's story reflects a lifetime of placing all her cares and hopes in God and her beloved Jesus Christ. At this particularly crucial time, she trusted God when everything pointed to hopelessness and destruction.

Inviting Louisa and Virginia to pray together brought unity and agreement in the Spirit, multiplying the power of God to move on Louisa's behalf. It is true that God can heal sovereignly, and sometimes He does. However, His design primarily involves His servants and friends on earth to pray together to proclaim healing from heaven for one another.

Initially, I felt led to pray simply for strength, comfort and peace for Louisa which was a necessary foundation for the later deeper healing of the cancer. Even in the face of looming death, Louisa kept her hope in her God as she had her whole life. She fought against fear and instead leaned into God's assurance of comfort and care. As she reflected in the end, she knew her Lord never took His eyes off of her. As she set her face toward Him, trusting in Him, He rescued her from death's door.

SCRIPTURES:

Romans 12: 15 Rejoice with those who rejoice, and weep with those who weep. NKJV

Psalm 33: 18–20 Behold the eye of the Lord is on those who fear Him, on those who hope in His mercy, to deliver their soul from death, and to keep them alive in famine. Our soul waits for the Lord; He is our help and our shield. NKJV

1 Peter 5: 6–8 Therefore humble yourselves under the mighty hand of God, that He may exalt you in due time, casting all your care upon Him, for He cares for you. Be sober, be vigilant; because your adversary the devil walks about like a roaring lion, seeking whom he may devour. NKJV

Isaiah 41:10 Fear not, for I am with you; be not dismayed, for I am your God. I will strengthen you, yes, I will help you, I will uphold you with My righteous right hand. NKJV

11

A SMILE IN THE SPIRIT

I gripped the steering wheel and stared blankly through the windshield. *I'm gonna be late. I just can't do this.* I lowered my head. A tear trickled down my cheek. Personal matters were weighing heavily on me. Anguished thoughts raced through my mind. *Maybe I should cancel, but I postponed her last week. I've got to go.* I glanced in the rearview mirror. "Mascara's smeared. Great, just what I need," I moaned. I grabbed a tissue for a quick repair. I was still weepy from last night's cry. I looked puffy and haggard.

"I have nothing to give, God," I muttered, more to myself than to Him, but I drew a deep breath and turned the key. As I drove, I couldn't even muster my usual fervent prayers. I felt listless and distracted. I reigned in my thoughts trying to focus on my appointment with Hannah. Awful stories cascaded through my mind. All five specialists said it. *She runs screaming and crying into a corner. Fussy. Whiny. They get nowhere with her.* "Jesus, I can't do this, not today!" I shouted. I struck the steering wheel for emphasis, but continued to drive.

I reviewed in my mind reports I'd read. *Born with hydrocephaly. Significant fluid on the brain. At three and a half years, has no words-- just a few sounds. She plays like a 16 month old and drops toys more than plays with them.*

Won't hold a cup or a spoon and walks with a left leg limp. She doesn't let you touch her. Seems afraid of everything and everyone. I groaned loudly.

I flashed on a recent meeting I'd attended where the principal of Hannah's preschool, Ms. Addison, submitted a request for a para-professional for Hannah.

She said Hannah needed one-on-one help. The teachers were all complaining about her constant crying and melt-downs. Ms. Addison said they needed someone assigned solely to Hannah in order to allow her to continue in the school. *Oh, Lord Jesus! I need an assistant myself today!* Hopelessness rose. I blew out a deep breath of exhaustion and dread.

I sensed the Holy Spirit's still small voice. 'Put in a worship tape and sing along.' I recognized the leading of the Lord. But even so, I begrudgingly responded, slipping a tape into the player. I lacked any genuine faith. As the worship song resounded through the car, I repeated the lyrics in a detached monotone. My feelings did not match the high intensity zeal of the worshippers on the tape, but I forced out the phrases, "I sing for joy at the work of Your hands, forever I'll love you, forever I'll stand. Nothing compares to the promise I have in you...my Jesus, my Savior..."

I pulled up to their small home in a deteriorating neighborhood. Shutting off the cassette player, I solemnly gathered my notebook and evaluation materials. "This is not going to be pretty," I mumbled to myself. But I sent up a quick prayer, saying: "God, I've got nothing to give. You got me here, so please help me!" To my surprise, a portion of scripture flashed through my mind. 'You are the Vine, I am the branch, I can do nothing without You, but as You dwell in me and I dwell in You, You bring forth much fruit.'

To my surprise, I caught a quick vision of me walking hand-in-hand with Jesus. "OK Lord, walk through that door with me," I prayed aloud. "Let that child see You and not me!" After locking the car door behind me, I discretely reached out a hand and imagined Jesus slipping His hand into mine, guiding me across the street. I walked like a child following her daddy.

Dragging my feet, I slowly climbed the decaying porch steps. I knocked. No one answered. I turned to go, relieved. But behind me I heard the old pine door creak open. My heart sank. I threw on a smile before turning back to say, a little too happily, "Hi, I'm Anita, the occupational therapist." A stocky woman in her forties standing no more than 5 feet tall peeked out. She looked as hesitant as I felt. As she cautiously opened the door, I caught a glimpse of a little girl who I guessed was Hannah standing in the kitchen doorway clutching a woman's leg.

Stepping over the threshold into their hallway, I noticed Hannah had disappeared into the kitchen. I prayed silently as I chatted with Rose, Hannah's mom who introduced me to her sister, Aunt Cynthia. I saw out of the corner of my eye, a little brunette head peer back around the door at me. I prayed in a whisper, "Help us, Jesus!" I turned toward the kitchen with the best smile I could manufacture.

"Oh, you must be Hannah!" Our eyes met. There was a poignant moment where everyone stood frozen. I watched, as if in slow motion, as Hannah's frowning little face and tightly drawn down mouth, slowly curled up into a huge smile. Suddenly, amazing all of us, especially me, Hannah raised her little arms and set out rushing straight at me. As I saw her barreling toward me, I instinctively lowered one knee to the floor to receive her. She flung her arms around my neck. Her impact was so exuberant, she almost knocked me over. As we gave each other a deep joyful hug, I felt her plant a big kiss on my cheek. Best kiss ever. I laughed, awestruck and overjoyed. Squeals of laughter erupted from Rose.

"Well hello Hannah!" I exclaimed. Hannah giggled and nuzzled her dark curls into my neck and shoulder, allowing me to pick her up to swing her around.

"Wow! Well, she sure likes you!" Rose exclaimed. "She usually runs screaming and hides in the bathroom."

"Yeah, never saw that before!" Cynthia said rather cynically.

My first thought, *'oh, you have no idea! It was not me!'* I knew sweet Hannah by the grace of God had sensed Jesus' presence. Later reflecting on it, I realized that when I slid my hand through Jesus hand - that became a spiritual reality. Children are very sensitive in the Spirit and when I walked through that door, Hannah's little spirit attuned to Jesus' beautiful Spirit and it was His Spirit of Love to which she was magnetized, not mine. I was certain of that.

After a moment, she scrambled out of my arms to the floor. Just like we were best friends, she grabbed my hand and led me into the living room. A bewildered Rose and Cynthia trailed. I was stunned but hung onto her tiny hand, so grateful to God.

Rose saw me take notice of Hannah's lurching gait and offered, "She's had that hip problem since she was born. She gets around pretty good now. Took her a long time to walk but always has limped like that."

Hannah and I nestled down on the floor, next to the couch. I dug quickly into my test kit trying not to lose the momentum. I pulled out pegboards and shape puzzles, placing them between us. Hannah stared at the toys, but didn't budge. Rose sat on the couch near us, leaning forward, elbows on her knees, watching every move. Cynthia lagged behind and found a chair at the far end of the room. She leaned back crossing her arms; her glasses rested low on her nose as she scrutinized me.

"Look Hannah," I said. "See how the circle piece fits into the circle hole?" I asked. "Can you try it, honey?" as I held the circle block out to her.

You could almost hear the 'hrumph' from Aunt Cynthia echo across the room. I knew Cynthia was highly suspicious about this whole thing. I couldn't blame her. She had seen so many specialists and nurses come and go as her precious niece huddled in a corner screaming and crying.

Seated on the floor near me, Hannah rotated on her bottom and turned her back on me. She solemnly stared off. I thought, *Uh-oh, she's getting ready to bolt.* I prayed silently. But then slowly, she turned her head and looked at me over her shoulder. Her intent stare turned into a broad smile. Rotating back to me, she reached out and took the circle block. Exploring the piece for a moment, she took my hand and placed it over hers, so my hand could guide hers. Together, we slid the circle piece into its place.

"Good job, Hannah! Wow, look what we did," I encouraged enthusiastically.

"Yay!" Rose exclaimed, shooting a look to Cynthia, "Did you see that? She usually just drops puzzle pieces, right Cynthia?"

Cynthia arose to take a closer look. Little Hannah beamed up at her aunt. "Now look what you went and did, little girl," Cynthia teased. "Auntie's so proud of you." Ruffling Hannahl's hair, she took a seat next to Rose showing renewed interest.

I could see Jesus actively at work with this child, right before our eyes. I was overwhelmed by His show of love. Clearly, there was an atmosphere of awe and optimism. Rose and Cynthia smiled and nodded as we joyfully proceeded with the tests.

Hannah's lilting laughter wafted through the house like a fresh rain as I presented stacking blocks, balls, crayons and paper. Hannah seemed delighted by her successes and excited with new challenges. Amazingly, she even allowed me to lead her through several tests assessing her strength, joint stability and movement patterns. I scribbled notes feverishly on forms, trying not to lose her attention, noting muscle weakness, abnormal reflexes and a left hip tightness causing a significant limp.

About a half hour into the session, Rose and Cynthia were called out of the room. I felt relieved to have a little time alone with Hannah. I guided her through a final task of stringing wooden beads. Seated in my lap with my arm draped around her shoulders, she let me help her. I took the moment to pray over her, quietly thanking the Lord Jesus for what He had done and asking Him to heal her body, soul and spirit.

I was stooping over my bag, packing up my equipment when Rose returned with two cups of coffee.

"Thank you. I can use that," I said.

I took a sip as I gazed across the room at a playful happy Hannah retrieving a ball. I smiled, grateful for all that God had done, but also grateful that the session was winding down. Rose was positioning coasters on a table behind me as I continued to sip and watch Hannah. As I stood watching, I blinked. *No, I didn't just see that!* My full coffee cup wobbled in my hands. I swallowed hard. I choked a bit. I blinked again and craned my neck, taking a step toward Hannah to get a closer look. *No, surely, I must be imagining, it couldn't be….*

I said almost audibly, "Oh, Jesus. Thank you, Jesus." My mind raced ahead. *But how am I going to explain this?* I questioned.

I could hardly believe my eyes, but Hannah was walking with no trace of a limp. Her gait was completely smooth and normal for her age. Stunned but composing myself, I heard myself ask Rose.

"Say, by the way, which leg did you say was tighter?" I asked. I had a sense to let mom discover the change. Or maybe I needed the witness of another to get over my own shock. But for whatever reason, that's what I said.

Rose and I looked on together as Hannah pursued the rolling ball. Rose watched her daughter trundle across the room. Shaking her head, Rose bent at the waist to get a better look. I could see she looked a bit baffled.

"Umm, I forget sometimes which leg it is, but I think it's her...." Rose gawked at her daughter. She hurried across the room, looking from several angles. Then she just stopped in her tracks and watched her child walking with ease across the room. Rose's face sobered.

"She's not doing it now. She's just not...." Her voice now rising to a high-pitched shrill, "She's not limping!"

"Cynthia, Cynthia, come here! She's not limping! Come see this!" Cynthia, still occupied with a phone call, thankfully didn't hear her which gave Rose and me a moment to process what we were seeing.

Wide-eyed, Rose stuttered, "What happened? How come?" Still trying to recover and gather my thoughts, I just shook my head and prayed silently: What do I say, Father? Show me what to say?

Then what came out was: "You pray for Hannah, right?" I'm not sure how I knew that, but I did, which had to be revelation from the Lord.

She nodded, "Yes."

"Well, I pray for children too, and sometimes Jesus heals them."

Rose kept shaking her head. Scooping Hannah in her arms, kissing her repeatedly on her smiling cheek, they walked me to the door.

"Thank you, thank you so much!" Rose kept repeating. Clearly we were both stunned and there was little that could be said. However we did make sure we honored the One who deserves the glory, "Let's just both thank Jesus. He's the healer," I smiled as we hugged.

Embracing her beloved daughter in her arms, they waved exuberantly from the door. As I left, I was virtually airborne all the way to my car, so different from my arrival. I ran across the street, shocked and elated. I was anxious to call a faithful prayer warrior who always awaited news of breakthroughs with my patients. I slipped my cassette tape into the player and worshiped enthusiastically all the way home.

Following that session, everything shifted for little Hannah. Hannah stopped limping that day and it was documented by her doctors. She never limped again. But the resolving of her hip tightness and the limp was apparently only the tip of the iceberg. After that amazing day, Hannah worked with all of her teachers and specialists with joy and cooperation. The speech therapist began making great headway with her. I necessarily kept a low profile about the event but watched the unfolding fruit of God's touch on this little one.

All her teachers and therapists echoed similar reports: 'engaging well in tasks, smiling, and content, happy and compliant through sessions.' People tried to discover if there had been a change of medications or a shift in the home environment, but no shifts could be identified. I knew the only difference was the powerful touch from a loving Father God who knew how to meet and heal His child.

Visiting Hannah at her school in the following weeks, I heard these comments from various staff:

- "She is such a joy!" her preschool teacher exclaimed. "A light just seemed to come on!"

- "I used to spend most of the day just trying to get her to try anything new. Most days she was frustrated and whined all day," shared one of the teacher aides. "Now she's a delight, one of my easiest children."

- "She's so cooperative now. It's hard to believe that she is the same child," shared a co-teacher.

- "I don't think of myself as having favorites and try not to, but Hannah is just special. She makes me smile. Her mom needed someone to keep her late because of her work and I jumped at the chance. She's my special little buddy," commented the school principal.

- "Oh, Hannah just seems to enjoy learning now," shared a learning specialist.

Hannah made rapid gains over the next months of her treatment. All of her specialists spoke of her dramatic changes. A common story was told about how Hannah, who had been such a whiny, fussy and dependent child, now beamed happiness and delight. She had become a most magnetic child, who shined the radiant countenance of God. Remembering back to that first very amazing day, I knew we both were touched, never to be the same again. That is the Lord's trademark of His completed work, His joy and His peace for everyone involved.

REFLECTIONS:

I dreaded walking into their home that day with such a difficult case as this. Distraught, hopeless and oppressed myself, I cried out to the

Lord. I was certain nothing of value could come of this visit in my state of mind. I asked the Lord to hold my hand as I walked through this visit. I was only beginning to understand that when we feel the most broken with nothing to give, God can work most mightily through us.

In that home, everything had been tried. Talented specialists were sent but the God of Glory who loved Hannah, knew how to meet and restore her. The prayers of a faithful mom who never stopped hoping and praying got heaven's attention and response. Then it was orchestrated to send in one who had nothing but one thing, awareness that she needed Jesus to take her hand and walk her through a door.

SCRIPTURES:

Zechariah 4:6 "This is the word of the LORD to Zerubbabel: 'Not by might nor by power, but by My Spirit,' Says the LORD of hosts." NKJV

John 15:5 "I am the vine, you are the branches. He who abides in Me, and I in him, bears much fruit; for without Me you can do nothing." NKJV

2 Corinthians 12: 9-10 And He said to me, "My grace is sufficient for you, for My strength is made perfect in weakness." Therefore most gladly I will rather boast in my infirmities, that the power of Christ may rest upon me. Therefore I take pleasure in infirmities, in reproaches, in needs, in persecutions, in distresses for Christ's sake. For when I am weak, then I am strong. NKJV

12

FROM STROKE TO SUCCESS

After 70 active years of living life fully, Caroline entered an era of three years of warring for survival after her massive stroke. Sitting motionless in her living room lounge across from me, she still managed to flash a weak but hopeful smile. Her silvery gray hair framed lovely blue eyes which mirrored her pure heart. But her weariness reflected her battle fatigue. Throughout her life, she was known for her kindness, giving gifts of her famous cornbread, sworn by most as the best in Huberville. However, when the stroke hit three years earlier and she lost her ability to speak and move her left side, nothing was ever the same.

In the first weeks of our homebound therapy visits, Andy, her exuberant loving husband asked me to help Caroline prepare some of her cornbread. Unfortunately, as she sat at the table, it became quickly evident that all the ingredients from the midpoint of her body to the left were virtually invisible to her. Her eyes just couldn't move or perceive things in that direction. Scrambling, so as not to discourage her, I pressed through the baking activity. It was apparent that as her left arm and leg lay limp and orphaned from the rest of her; it impeded all two-sided ventures, resulting in total dependency. She needed help to walk, dress, and bath, reliant upon Andy and her home health aides for everything.

It was so heartbreaking, because it seemed about everyone in their small town owned a crocheted scarf or hat, a 'Caroline Creation.' For years, Andy had been entrusted to keep the aging Ford Taurus named Nellie, tuned up and ready to roll. You never knew when Caroline would need to respond to a neighbor's call. But from that traumatic day forward, Nellie, much like Caroline, came to a screeching halt.

Caroline's adult children, Nancy and Rob came to check on their parents regularly. Though they greeted cheerily with hugs, just beneath the surface, I sensed that something indescribable had been lost. I watched as interactions with Caroline seemed flat and expressionless, just like the left side of her body which lay lifeless and unreachable.

At one of my early visits, an aide retrieved Caroline's old crochet basket from her closet after Caroline pointed to it. Her caregiver compassionately placed it near Caroline's lounge chair. As I came and went, the old wilting skeins of unused yarn yawned over the edge of her dusty brown woven friend that had been her constant traveling companion. My heart was gripped as I saw Caroline extend a longing gaze at her basket, then expel a sigh of resignation as her eyes drifted back to her new best friend – the TV. It was simple. It didn't demand much and Andy was so faithful to sit in his chair so near to watch and doze with her. Hours a day sitting spellbound before the TV turned into months, then years. This TV ritual had been interrupted only by periodic intervals of visits by speech and physical therapists who tried to arouse old neurologic muscle and sensory memory patterns, but to no avail. Now it was my turn. And frankly, I was worried.

"I wish I could just chat with her," her daughter Nancy, shared privately, "about anything really, but she can't get the words out. We don't want to frustrate her, so we just ask her yes or no questions...." Nancy's voice faded.

"I can only imagine what a loss this must be for you," I empathized.

"Even after all this time," she said clearing her throat, "I miss our talks. I can see it makes her sad too," as she reached for a tissue from her purse.

At our following session, I tapped at the door of their brick ranch. As always, I got the usual welcome. "So how's Anita today?" roared Andy's familiar, friendly greeting as he flung open the screen door.

"Guess who's here, Caroline?" Leaning his 6' 3" lanky frame down toward me for an Andy bear hug, he said, "How are you?" He repeated it, exploring the details of a sincere response. I suppressed a slight gasp under his powerful hug. I smiled somewhat from relief as he released me, but down deep I enjoyed the Papa type attention.

He nearly shouted from the dining area toward her lounge chair in the parlor, "Anita's going to take her son to the beach next week, Caroline. Isn't that great? She's a good mom, isn't she honey? Yes, she is!" As a single parent I was grateful for his upbeat encouragement and was always struck by how he wove Caroline into most every conversation.

In the privacy of their kitchen, however, Andy gazed into the distance and wistfully recalled, "You know, Nita," he called me by my nickname, "I sure wish I could see her put on her sweater again with such flair, the way she did since she was a little girl." He grinned romantically. "When we met at Stradford Elementary, she'd take her sweater by the shoulders, like this." He demonstrated with an imaginary sweater mid-air, as he continued, "she'd twirl it 'round in front her, over her head to land square on her shoulders. Just loved that. Did it her whole life." He smiled in sweet recollection. "I sure do miss her cornbread; the smell used to fill the whole house." His tender smile morphed into a frown. "Why has God allowed this?" he spoke almost inaudibly, for the hundredth time, I was sure.

When Andy's riding lawn mower kicked into full gear that day, with the "rhm-rhm-rhmmmm" jarring the quiet, I was determined to 'have that chat' with Caroline. I chose my words carefully, speaking slowly, tenderly.

"Caroline honey, I see your Bible sitting out and that beautiful picture of Jesus in the dining room. Are you still praying for Jesus to heal you?" Her bowed head jolted upright; she stared directly into my stunned face. Her normal pallid complexion washed into a rich rosy hue. Her eyes widened as she vigorously nodded her head.

I heard myself saying, amazed by my own lips forming the words, "Would you like me to pray with you for healing?" Her broad smile and moist eyes answered the question.

Later I slipped into my Toyota Corolla, glanced into my rear view mirror and looked over my shoulder, as I backed out of their driveway. I caught the metaphor and thought, *There's no turning back now, Anita.* I had wondered some weeks before about broaching this subject of healing with Caroline, but thought, *Are you crazy, Anita? Are you getting way out there?*

I prayed as I drove slowly out of their quiet neighborhood gripping the steering wheel as if somehow clutching Jesus himself. "Oh God, help her. Heal her. Restore her. We have nothing but you!" I prayed as I drove.

I knew from years of experience, change in function three years past the original stroke was not considered feasible. But something was happening with me that I could not ignore. Recently when I would pray for Caroline, I had been catching a glimpse in my mind's eye of her walking down her hallway, getting out of her chair by herself, and even crocheting a little again. I was learning to trust God that when he showed me things like this, He was showing me His heart and plan for my patient if I could only believe. I was learning to trust Him that He was asking me to pray in agreement with what I was seeing.

The following sessions, I initiated a program of activities which included prayer and mental imagery involving the use of both sides of her body. The Lord had shown me that as we prayed and trusted God together, my patients' imaginations could be sanctified by Him. He would then help them see and believe for abilities and function to return, making possible what seemed impossible to glorify Him and to bless them.

"Catch the ball Caroline." I said, as the huge 15 inch ball bounced toward her while she sat in her sofa chair. "Use both hands, Caroline. Close your eyes for a minute like I showed you. Ask Jesus to help you to remember how to do it!"

I stopped the activity for a moment and raised her arms, wrapping them carefully around the ball; she needed help to feel and grip the large ball. "That's right, Caroline," I encouraged. "Ask Jesus to help you imagine how it would look and feel to catch the ball using your right and left arms."

She paused. I watched her lips move silently, "Show me Jesus. Thank you Jesus." Then she opened her eyes and tried it. I was stunned to see in the very next toss of the ball toward her, that her left arm and hand rose ever so slightly from her lap to assist her right side to catch the ball. Once – twice – then 10 -15 times, her left side seemed to gradually be 'waking up.'

Over the next 10 minutes, I was awed as I watched. With each bounce of the ball toward her, inch by inch, her left side became more and more engaged. We stopped intermittently to have her close her eyes, pray and imagine with Jesus. We were stunned. Something very new was happening. I knew it. I could tell she knew it. A smile washed over her lovely face as fresh hope surfaced. We stopped. We stared at each other.

"Wow!" I expressed in amazement. Her wide eyed smile of agreement silently spoke, 'We're onto something big here, aren't we!' Slowly over many consecutive sessions, her left side assisted the right more and more, first in catching balls, then in crossing her body to stack or retrieve rings or blocks and finally clapping her hands on her knees in time to songs.

With each task, she would faithfully close her eyes, ask Jesus for help as she imagined and tried new feats. We prayed. We agreed. We prayed some more for Jesus' power to heal and restore. I watched the beginning of a new era. A fresh peace washed over her as we prayed. New hope arose. I knew I was watching God's grace and mercy unfolding before us.

"Help me Jesus!" and then "Thank you, Jesus!" were some of her first short sentences, breaking years of silence.

"Look right here, Caroline," I said, hoping to build her faith. "See in the Book of John, chapter 5, right here in your own Bible, Jesus did the same thing we're doing when He walked the earth. He just saw what the Father in heaven was already doing and then He just agreed with it, speaking it out, giving Him the glory."

Two months later, I was doing some retesting to gauge how she was doing. "Ouch!" she yelped, as she swiped a playful slap at my poke to her leg. She felt the pain as I tested for leg sensations. With glee, she heartily returned my hug because she knew this was a milestone. Years of deadened sensation on her left side was breaking free to new feelings and movement.

I stood behind her, moving my tiny flashlight near her eyes on the left. "Can you see this?" I queried. "Tell me when you can see the light," as I tested for peripheral vision.

"Yes, Yes." she'd respond or raise her hand to signal me. She was tracking light with her eyes further and further to the left with each week's visit. More breakthroughs! We were delighted.

During dressing practice, we also saw gains. "That's right," I said, trying to encourage her every step of the way. "Ask Jesus to help you use your left hand to help with that button, Caroline! Close your eyes. Imagine it and then try it." A frustrated, "whew" escaped her determined lips at these times. But Caroline was a fighter and she'd close her eyes, ask Jesus for help and persevere.

Sometimes while her aide was helping her down the hallway, I'd encourage Caroline to talk to her lagging left leg. "That's right, Caroline! Tell that left leg to line up and do its part."

Caroline would glance up at me and chortle, "That's good, Nita! Thank you, Jesus!" For a lady who had stopped talking three years back, this was so sweet to hear.

She was beginning to beam most days as the radiance of her deepened intimacy with God and renewed hope poured from her countenance. Her family noticed.

"You're lookin' beee-u-tee-ful darling," bellowed Andy as he moved in and out of the living room dramatically applauding her fervent efforts. He would often reach down to give her a tender hug before he'd leave the room, shaking his head in wonder and gratitude at his wife's weekly gains.

Then the victory we'd all awaited, her first slow unassisted journey down their 20-foot hallway. The gala event was enjoyed by Andy, me and a home health aide, all acting as her personal cheerleading section. In moments, like a fawn struggling to find its newborn legs, she waddled and weaved toward Andy. His broad grin and outstretched arms motivated his beloved to stay the course. She steadied herself with an occasional arm against a wall, more for reassurance than needed support, as her fans hooted and clapped with excitement.

"You can do it! That's it! You're almost there!" We took turns exclaiming.

Her goal was to reach Andy's loving arms. In her last few steps, she rushed into his enthusiastic embrace. Lifting her off the ground, Andy planted a loud kiss on her cheek, easing her into a chair for a much deserved rest. With smiles and laughs, cutting huge slabs of a chocolate layer cake through misting eyes, he croaked, "It's been the day of days! By God's good grace, we've come a long ways. I so-o-o appreciate what you've all done for me and my sweetie!" shooting Caroline an adoring look.

Then the day of the great report came. After returning from her six-month physician's checkup, her son, Rob shared this sweet story:

"So I helped her walk into the doc's office. She insisted on leaving her walker in the car. Wasn't havin' any of that! Then with a big old grin on her face, she handed the doc that crocheted doily she's been working on. Ha!" I smiled, imagining Dr. Pritchard's shock and joy for his patient.

"Then Dad gave him a big old slice of that cornbread he and mom made last week and the doc could hardly believe his eyes. It was fun to watch! After his exam, mom thanked him, grabbed her sweater from dad and flipped it over her head in that twirling thing she does! The doc about lost it. Dad just said, 'Ever seen anything like that?' Course mama, she just kept saying, 'Thank you Jesus, thank you Jesus.' Dr. Pritchard wanted to know who's been working with her. When we reminded him it was you, Anita, he just said, 'Well, whatever she's doing tell her to keep doing it!' So I told him I'd let you know."

And so we followed the doctor's orders. We prayed. We trusted. We walked out the reality of her healing by the hand of a good and faithful God.

On one of my last visits, her daughter, Nancy came to me saying, "I can't tell you how wonderful it is to have simple sweet talks with mom. Last week she even asked me about me and the family. Thank you for helping me have more of Mom back, Anita." Then she glanced up and said, "And thank you, Jesus."

REFLECTIONS:

Caroline hung on with just a shred of hope and faith for healing. Her family still longed for the mother and wife they remembered, continuing to pray for her. God took Caroline's weak faith and her buried desire, multiplying and blessing back to her as an ever faithful God. He loves to give His beloved children the desires of their hearts. Inside her quiet demeanor, Caroline had never given up. She just needed someone to come alongside to believe with her.

We are encouraged that if we have faith like a mustard seed, we can move mountains. The mustard seed is one of the tiniest seeds on earth, however when planted and crushed it becomes one of the most potent and strong seeds. In Israel, the mustard seed, though tiny and weak in appearance, has been known to mature into one of the hardiest herbal plants in that region, growing up to twelve feet tall and able to be a nesting place for birds. So to 'have faith as a mustard seed' is to take our tiny seed of faith and allow it to be multiplied by the God who is ever faithful to allow us to be blessed and be a blessing, far beyond what appears possible.

SCRIPTURES:

Matthew 17:20 So Jesus said to them...."for assuredly, I say to you, if you have faith as a mustard seed, you will say to this mountain, 'Move from here to there,' and it will move; and nothing will be impossible for you." NKJV

Psalm 37: 3-4 Trust in the Lord and do good; dwell in the land, and feed on His faithfulness. Delight yourself also in the Lord, And He shall give you the desires of your heart. NKJV

Psalm 31:24 Be of good courage, And He shall strengthen your heart, all you who hope in the Lord. NKJV

2 Corinthians. 5:7 For we walk by faith, not by sight. NKJV

13

RESCUED FROM RESTRICTIONS

Peggy Crandel clutched my shirt sleeve as she steered me down the wide stucco-walled corridor toward her preschool classroom. The rapid clicking of our heels echoed off the old hardwood floors as we hurried along. The urgent journey followed my one quick nod of my head indicating my willingness to look at a child in her class for whom she expressed serious concerns. Lowering her voice to a near whisper as we entered her classroom, Ms. Crandel protected our conversation from unwanted ears.

"Mary's been in my class for over six months, Anita. I've never seen her walk. She's three years old!" as she leaned in closer and gripped my arm for emphasis. "I've seen her try to pull herself up from the floor next to a table a couple of times, but she just flops down." Shaking her head in silent desperation, Peggy paused. She released her tight grip on my shirt sleeve and pointed toward a tiny blonde in pigtails sitting on the floor wistfully playing with a mini xylophone.

"I just thought, well you know, maybe you could just take a quick look and see what you think. Would you mind?" Her fervor was compelling. I smiled. I closed my eyes for a brief reflective prayer and knew by the inner peace I felt, that this was a divine appointment. "Sure Peggy. I'd be happy to."

Peggy was a smart dedicated teacher. She knew the protocol. She knew full well that she was stretching the rules a bit, by inviting a therapist to give an opinion on a child without an official referral, but as she explained, she had tried everything. "Thank you so much!" I could sense her gratitude and relief that a bridge was in sight over what seemed like an ever widening chasm that she feared would eventually swallow up any hope for this child. The weight she had been carrying lifted for a moment as we heaped her burden on shared shoulders. I learned later that the circulating stories of some of the miraculous healings and recovery of children under my care had driven Peggy to this request.

"Her legs just look so thin and scrawny to me," Peggy worried. "I tried to get her mom to take her to the doctor. Spoke to her three different times about it. She promised, but it never happened. Mom's young and overwhelmed and well, you know…."

We approached little Mary as she continued tapping the musical keys with her wooden mallet. Peggy stooped next to her saying, "Hi honey, this is my friend, Miss Anita. She's come to play with you for a few minutes. Can you say hi?"

Her pigtails bounced slightly as she nodded, looking up at me flashing a set of sparkling green eyes and a welcoming smile. I joined them by taking a seat on the floor. Mary and I took turns with the mallet on the xylophone creating sweet refrains of 'Mary had a little lamb.' Peggy joined in with a mini tambourine as back up rhythm. We all giggled together enjoying our simple band ensemble.

"Hey, Mary, want to sit on the table over there?" Again, a nod and a smile signaled me to scoop her up and carry her to a nearby dressing table. While she sat on the edge of the table, I superficially examined her legs. Peggy handed her a favorite toy bunny to cuddle. We exchanged kisses and hugs with the bunny before I began a brief exam.

Years as a therapist let me see and feel quickly that her thigh and calf muscles were weak and spongy to the touch. Her hip and knee joints were also very loose and unstable. Tucking my hands under her arms, I hiked her up into a standing position, keeping a solid hold on her hips. I knew she would have collapsed quickly without this extra firm support.

By now, we had attracted the attention of three other teachers' aides who gathered behind us to watch. Apparently, there were others in this preschool room who shared Peggy's concerns for little Mary.

Trying not to become distracted, but aware of the audience now forming behind me, I held Mary in this standing position in front of me. I prayed quietly asking for God's mercy, love and strengthening for Mary. Silently, I cried out for the Holy Spirit to manifest and heal as I claimed the blood and authority of Jesus over sweet Mary. Standing face to face with her now, Mary and I looked directly and deeply into one another's eyes. I whispered under my breath "Jesus, lay your precious hands upon this child; have mercy on her and heal her." I smiled at her and held her upright like this for two to three minutes. I sensed God's presence and His peace surrounding and enfolding us.

By a leading of the Holy Spirit, I simply began to stroke Mary's tiny weak legs from her hips down to her ankles. I stroked the length of her legs from her hips to ankles several times, pressing down through her wobbly hips, quickly replacing my hands on her hips to keep her from falling. I repeated this pattern numerous times.

Suddenly, I detected the most amazing phenomenon as I stroked and prayed and stroked and prayed. I could feel with each sweep of my hands that the weak spongy muscles of her thighs and calves were firming up and even becoming plumper and more solid. Astonishing! But there was no question that her actual little legs were changing under my hands. I could hardly believe it but my trained hands could feel the very real shifts in the tone and size of the muscles. The Lord was moving.

I cautiously, but intentionally, lifted my hands away from Mary; to our amazement she remained standing. Even though, my faith has soared seeing so many miracles of healing, the Lord's awesome love and mercy never ceases to both bless and astound me. I stood amazed.

Mary remained standing. I thanked Him. Mary remained standing. My heart leapt. Mary remained standing and then she leaned forward and hugged me. Silently, we bystanders waited, hoping and praying as she held her stance. The entire time, Mary amused herself with her fluffy bunny, as her mesmerized audience beheld what could only be marked as an act of God.

I returned to stroking her little legs. From hips to ankles, I praised and stroked those unused muscles, worshipping the Lord within my spirit. I could feel her legs continue to strengthen beneath my fingers. Joints stabilized and muscles firmed still further. The therapy years had sensitized my hands to the nuances of muscular change; and, the transformation of the muscular tone and the joint strength under my fingers was distinct and clear.

With a wide smile and eyes focused up toward mine, a table for her stage, Mary attempted a couple of tentative but very clear steps. No one spoke. I scooped her up, bunny and all, setting her on her feet on the floor below. To our delight, she hugged her bunny and then took five more steps. On the fifth miraculous step, Mary dropped her toy but instinctively squatted down and retrieved him. This stunned me as squatting and returning to stand would normally take weeks to develop for a new walker.

A hush filled the room and we beamed witnessing this great awakening. She took no special notice of her feat, but resumed her attention to her bunny as she left her assiduous audience in a wake of wonderment and awe. We didn't speak. With grateful hearts, we simply smiled at each other knowing we had just shared a touch from God on a child's life.

Weeks later, passing Peggy in the hall, I inquired about how Mary was doing.

Peggy bubbled, "Just wonderful, she is walking more and more each day. She'll be off and running soon!"

To God, be the glory!

REFLECTIONS:

Watching her beloved student struggle brought Peggy to a point of anxiety and fear. It is understandable when such a dire situation persists. But when God was sought in prayer and gratitude, He moved on this little one's behalf, responding as well to alleviate the concerns of the classroom staff. The merciful heart of God moved in a moment, suddenly intervening, responding to the needs of everyone involved.

After this miraculous event, I was taken to that wonderful verse in scripture that promises that He allows us to mount up on wings like eagles, to run and not be weary, to walk and not faint. The kindness of God responded to the thoughts and prayers of many and met this child's needs. He is truly faithful. In one short moment, He drew a teacher and her staff into an entirely new place of faith and awesome wonder of God's mercy and love.

SCRIPTURES:

Philippians 4:6-7 Be anxious for nothing, but in everything by prayer and supplication, with thanksgiving, let your requests be made known to God;

and the peace of God, which surpasses all understanding, will guard your hearts and minds through Christ Jesus. NKJV

Isaiah 40:31 But those who wait on the Lord shall renew their strength; they shall mount up with wings like eagles, They shall run and not be weary, They shall walk and not faint. NKJV

Psalm 136:4 To Him who alone does great wonders, For His mercy endures forever; NKJV

Romans 8:28 And we know that all things work together for good to those who love God, to those who are called according to His purpose. NKJV

14

AWAKENING FROM ALZHEIMERS

I held Barbara's hand as I leaned toward her wheelchair. She needed comfort for her heart which was crippled with emotional pain. I spoke tenderly.

"It's okay dear, you can relax now. Everything's okay."
Silent for a moment, suddenly Barbara shook her head violently. Her large chest heaved. Then she erupted again.

"I'M NO GOOD!" she screamed. "You know -- EVERYBODY knows. The whole d--- WORLD KNOWS!"

A nurse's aide cautiously approached us, carrying fresh linens. She paused, shared a concerned glance toward me and then rubbed Barbara's shoulder.

"O-o-oh Barbara. We love you, sweetheart."
Barbara crouched. Leaning toward me and in a hushed tone, she said to me,

"These people come-n-go -- who are they?"

"That's Margie, your nurse's aide. She's here to change your sheets," I reassured. It was troubling because Barbara had enjoyed a pleasant interchange with Margie just thirty minutes earlier.

Slouching back, she scrutinized Margie suspiciously as she stripped her bed.

Margie, endeavoring to bring familiarity and recall into the conversation said, "Hey, Ms. Barbara, you know today is Tuesday, your regular shower day. I'll be back after lunch to get you."

Barbara's face softened in momentary recognition.

"I try to stand up -- they say I'll fall. I guess I do -- I don't know. I guess I'm just a d--- fool! That's what my husband says....."

The onset of mid-stage Alzheimer's disease was playing havoc with Barbara's mind and emotions. Things were getting worse. Her face contorted as she wove snippets of indiscernible phrases together. I reeled with desire to see the unbridled accusations stop and prayed she could be freed from her personal prison. Within her litany of fear and paranoia, she peered over my shoulder, apparently seeing a delusional vision.

"Get away Frank! Leave me alone!" she screamed as she cowered beneath an imaginary looming figure.

I leaned forward facing her eye to eye. "Barbara honey, you're safe now. No one can hurt you here," I said gently but firmly. Part of me wanted to run out of the room weeping. It was so hard to watch this attack on her soul.

I knew she was having yet another flashback of the many beatings she'd suffered in her marriage with Frank. The couple had been admitted to Crescent Manor together. Though initially they shared a room, due to their traumatizing arguments the staff was forced to separate them for their own safety and overall peace. They gave Frank a room on an adjacent wing.

I prayed silently as I stroked her arm. She seemed to respond well to the prayers. As usual, her breathing slowed and she leaned back in her wheelchair. She closed her eyes for a moment and as she opened them, she appeared to be entering into a new reality. She scanned the room. A slight smile crept across her face.

"You know we've lived here in this house for a long time."

"Really?" I said, entering her imaginary world to try to bring peace.

Nodding she continued. "We raised our kids here. It's a nice place." She looked admiringly around her scant and sterile room. I sighed knowing that she was once again confusing the facility for her former home of 40 years. Examining the room with her, I tried to envision what she was seeing.

Then abruptly, she broke her gaze to look back at me to say, "Do you have any popcorn? I like candy. Do you have some?"

Attempting to follow the abrupt shifting of gears, I said, "Well Barbara, let's see." I glanced at my watch. "Lunch will be here in 15 minutes and I think they're serving roast chicken, a favorite of yours, right?"

"Next time, bring some chocolate, ok? Will you come back?"

"Sure, Barbara I will be back. But the nurses tell me that you're on a special diabetic diet, so I can't bring candy."

With a glazed stare, she sped on.

"Yeah, those kids....don't come home from school on time.....trouble -- trouble...." With her head bowed now, she stared down at her lap as her words trailed off. Mumbling followed.

Trying to keep her engaged and focused, I asked, "So how many children do you have, dear?"

"Ah, children?.... do I have?..... oh, one time a girl came...I don't know...." She gazed anxiously out the window. My heart sank.

I watched her vacant eyes roam the courtyard of greenery out her window. A bird flew past. I reflected on how far Barbara's life had drifted from this picture of serenity and freedom. As I continued to solemnly consider this thought, I looked down and noticed that Barbara's right foot had slipped off the footrest. Sadly, she didn't seem to notice. Since the stroke she had suffered two years earlier, she was quite weak and couldn't feel much on her right side. To complicate matters, she gained a lot of weight from lack of exercise. Having repositioned her leg on the foot plate twice earlier, I realized that each time, she was gradually sliding down, slumping lower and lower until her right arm and hand hung precariously off the armrest.

Knowing the discomfort and potential danger of this position, I rose to boost her upright with Margie's help. Sitting back down, I clasped her right hand. I'd found that touch seemed to help her stay calmer and more alert. As she stared out of the window, however her right hand gradually squeezed firmer and firmer around mine. Unfortunately, her fingers tightened until she was holding mine in a vise-like grip. A mini-tug-of-war ensued. The harder I pulled, the tighter she gripped. Barbara was unaware.

Leaning toward her, I gently queried, "Can you open your hand, dear?" Stunned, she looked down at her hand, then up at me. In flushed helplessness, she said, "I'm sorry…I…I…don't…."

I smiled reassuringly, "It's all right, Barbara." Carefully I pried open her fingers one by one to release her grip.

As I left, Margie stopped me outside the room and said,

"I see you got 'The Grip.' Frowning in worry she said, "Her feeling on her right side is getting real bad."

She ushered me a few feet from the doorway and in a hushed tone, she said, "Showering is so hard now. Her whole right side is useless and she's so heavy. We've got to have three aides to move her now or she falls. Scares me."

Biting my lip, I said, "Oh, I can see that. I'm sure it's disturbing. I will definitely be working on increasing her awareness on her right side, but her anxiety is making it worse, isn't it?"

Margie nodded. "The nurse said we're gonna have to start using the Hoyer Lift if things don't change." This was a bad sign because using this large cloth basket and pulley device was typically a last resort for moving patients who no longer had the strength or body awareness to help in their own care.

The following week, I arrived for a third appointment with Barbara's daughter, Angela. She slid her petite frame into the sofa chair in the center's family room. Smoothing her skirt and taking a deep breath, she spoke slowly, apparently trying to subdue strong surfacing emotions.

"It's getting real tough." She looked down and then quickly away to hide welling tears. "This is hard to admit but mom...well, I know she...she doesn't always recognize me. Sometimes, I even can see....sometimes...she...she thinks I'm one of the staff." Her voice broke. With that final confession, her tiny shoulders shuddered a bit as tears streamed down her pallid cheeks. She reached for a tissue from the box I extended.

As she dabbed her face and eyes, she continued, "That really hurts."

"That's the hardest part, isn't it?" as I leaned toward her in empathy and comfort.

"I know she's glad to see me – well, sometimes. But lately she's so angry...."

Nodding in acknowledgment, I poured some coffee for her. As she took the cup from me, her hand shook. I quickly reached out to help steady it. We placed it together on the table next to her. Then vigorously shaking her head, a second cascade of tears poured forth. Her shoulders rocked as she sobbed bitter tears.

"Why me? Why us?" she choked out.

Carefully, I placed my hand on her shoulder offering consolation. My heart wrenched for all the loss and despair I'd seen this disease cause so many families.

Through sniffles, she said, "I'm sorry. I wasn't expecting...."

"It's okay, just let it out. It's normal for what you're going through."

Waiting until she calmed a bit, I asked, "How's the rest of the family doing?"

"Johnny, my younger brother stopped coming. He can't take it."

"I know that you're aware that this is part of the disease process, but that doesn't help much, does it?"

"I do know and I try not to take it personally...."

"It must be so very difficult," I offered tenderly, knowing little can console in these matters.

"And she's getting so weak. Anymore, it takes three people to move her. Will it just keep getting worse? Is there anything we can do?" She looked at me eagerly trying to find an answer beyond this misery.

"Well, there may be some things we haven't tried yet." I said.

I was thinking of the body awareness strategies that God had shown me to teach patients which involved using their imagination in conjunction with prayer. With God's help, I teach them to use their imaginations to move in ways they remember from the past, but that their bodies no longer moved volitionally. I had witnessed profound and unusual breakthroughs for many patients through this prayerful process. In this moment, however I surprised myself, that I was offering such encouragement given Barbara's extensive disabilities and diagnosis. I well knew the poor prognosis for an 85-year-old with Alzheimer's especially with such serious long-standing stroke symptoms of weakness and poor sensation.

"I could try teaching her a special mental imagery process that sometimes improves body awareness and function."

"Anything, please try anything. I never thought we would have to go through this. Sometimes I leave here so depressed."

Praying silently, I sensed God was inspiring me to see past apparent limits. In my mind's eye, I caught a quick picture of Barbara's smiling face as she sang hymns at the facility's Sunday church services. I also recalled how she calmed whenever I mentioned Jesus or spoke scriptures to her.

"You know, Angela I have noticed that your mom does seem to respond well to prayer and the Word of God."

"Really? How so?"

"When I mention the Lord Jesus, she calms down and talks about Him like an old friend. She also seems to really enjoy the Sunday services."

"Well, she loved her Bible." Glancing up, she seemed to be trying to catch a glimpse of a memory of her mom in earlier years. Smiling now, she said, "She did pray a lot."

"She told me she always prayed for your dad to be saved."

"Oh yes, that would be mom." Smiling she said, "Hmmm…maybe I should be praying for her more."

"We could pray together right now, if you'd like."

Her thoughtful steady nod signaled me to lead her in a short but potent prayer asking for Jesus to heal Barbara and to bring peace to Angela. She walked out that day with a visible lightness in her steps.

At Barbara's next session, while I stretched her right shoulder, I spoke encouraging scriptures softly into her ear. Again, it seemed to soothe her troubled mind and emotions.

"Jesus loves you with an everlasting love, Barbara. He will never leave you nor forsake you," I whispered.

Barbara took a breath. Her shoulders relaxed. "He is your Beloved and you are His." She leaned back in serenity as the words permeated her heart and soul.

Then Barbara offered, "I know Jesus loves me...and...and....I love Him. I'm grateful...for what He did on the Cross. You know He loves you too, right?"

"Yes I do, Barbara," I replied smiling, grateful to see her making a genuine heart-to-heart connection. I noticed a pooling of tears in her eyes as she repeated what she'd shared the week before.

"I always prayed for my husband, you know."

"Yes, you told me."

"I wish he could be saved. Prayed for him every night when he drove his truck."

Then she said, "I prayed for my children too. There is Johnny....I think....ah....yea, I think it's Johnny....and I have a girl....Angie...aaah...I mean....Angela....prayed for her too!"

After several weeks of speaking scriptures to her during our therapy sessions, I watched her slowly showing signs of peace of mind. She was thinking and speaking more clearly. Her closest aides noticed also and commented with surprise.

We all continued to express concern, however, about her flashbacks of beatings. Frank's occasional visits to her room continued to be fraught with distressing arguments which caused setbacks for Barbara.

The staff agreed that Barbara would benefit from being taught how to set healthier boundaries. I sensed I should try to discuss the matter with her.

"You know, Jesus gives us our hearts and our feelings, Barbara. He loves you and doesn't want to see you being hurt. Sometimes He wants us to tell people how we feel so they will treat us as we deserve. He wants us to respect ourselves and speak our truth in love. When we set a clear loving boundary, we show honor and respect for ourselves that also honors and respects others. They also need to see themselves as children of a loving God. Jesus wants the best for all of His children." Barbara listened intently.

"How do you feel when Frank visits and yells at you?" I asked.

"I don't like it. He SHOULDN'T do that. It makes me MAD."

"That's good Barbara to be in touch with your anger. That's a normal response for that situation. But it might be best if you didn't just yell back at him. Do you think you could tell him firmly but kindly how you are feeling? Jesus loves you. He wants Frank to treat you well and for you to speak your truth to Frank in love. You can't control how he'll respond when you tell him, but you will feel better about yourself if you don't argue back. What do you think?"

"I want him to stop but he says I yell at him too. Oh Jesus, forgive me for yelling at him. Help me Jesus." I could see she was starting to understand.

"Again Barbara, you can tell him firmly, but kindly, how you feel." I repeated to her for emphasis. "What could you say to him?"

"I could say, 'Frank, God loves me and you need to talk nice to me.' I probably should tell him that I'm sorry I yelled at him too, 'cause God loves him too."

Simple discussions like this one followed our prayer and therapy sessions. In a very amazing moment of courage and strength, she had an extraordinary interchange with Frank that she shared with me the following day.

"I just told him to treat me nice, Anita. I told him Jesus loves me and that Jesus loves him too. I told him I was sorry too. He didn't yell at me at all. We even laughed a little together. We never do that." Smiling, she was obviously strengthened and proud of herself.

During that same time period we were also working on increasing her body awareness, strength and sensation with deep touch and prayerful imagination work.

"Did you like that rubbing on your arms and legs, Barbara? That's a nice smelling lotion, isn't it?"

"Yes, I like it." She continued to rub her right leg. I was encouraged to see her gradually becoming more aware of her right leg and arm.

"Barbara, today I'll roll this big ball to you and you'll kick it back to me. First though, just close your eyes for a minute and imagine the ball rolling toward you. Just pretend you're kicking it back to me. Use your imagination. Can you see it?"

With her eyes closed she said, "Yes, yes I do."

"Okay, that's great. Now let's remember that Jesus never leaves us so He's right here with you. Try to sense Jesus' presence right near you helping you."

With her eyes still closed, she smiled broadly as she nodded.

"What's happening?"

"I imagined Jesus helping me and I kicked the ball to you."

"Great! Now imagine doing the same thing with your other leg." I walked over and rubbed her right leg to increase her awareness. As I repositioned myself across the room from her, I said, "OK, now open your eyes and do just what you saw yourself doing in your imagination. Let Jesus help you."

With focused intention, she kicked the ball -- first with her left foot, then her right. Alternating her feet, she repeated this process eight, nine, ten times. With each kick, the ball rolled further and further toward me.

"Excellent, Barbara!" I exclaimed. "Now let's bounce the big ball between us. Catch it with two hands like we practiced. First imagine it with Jesus helping. Remember to close your eyes and imagine catching it first. Then open your eyes and try it."

After imagining, Barbara eyes popped open. I bounced the ball toward her. She caught the ball and bounced it back to me. With each of eight bounces her right hand moved higher on the ball and engaged more naturally and solidly.

Over the next weeks of treatment, Barbara was obviously getting stronger and using the right side of her body more easily. The staff was able to help her with dressing and bathing with fewer concerns. We were grateful to see such steady improvements.

"Oh, sure, I can do that," as she took the brush from the aide and prettied herself in front of the mirror.

"You sure look nice today, Barbara," the aide complimented.

"Thank you. I might be getting some visitors today. Maybe my daughter Angela, or Frank might come."

Many things were changing, but I wasn't quite prepared for what occurred about three months into treatment. I arrived at the facility to hear about a rather astounding event. As I entered that day, I ran into one of the physical therapists in the hallway. She was quite excited and blurted out,

"Anita, what's that visualizing thing you're doing with Barbara?"

"Oh, you mean the mental imagery? Why do you ask?" I knew without Jesus presence being included that it would be a far less effective treatment. I was cautious to share this treatment approach with someone who may not understand the power of prayer and the ministry of healing through God.

"Just yesterday, Ms. Barbara walked the entire hallway, 75 feet down and 75 back with her walker. Her aide said she had good balance, only needed a couple of rests."

"Really? Wow, that's great!"

Thanking Jesus silently, I also wondered how the Lord would want me to respond to her question.

"So what do you do? I want to learn that technique!"

"Well, we do use imagination, but we always do this with prayer and asking Jesus for help. Barbara has a strong faith, you know."

"Yes, yes, but it must be that visualizing thing you're teaching her!"

With that response, I knew I needed time to think and pray. Thankfully I was actually rushing to a therapy appointment.

"Hey, Sandy, could we catch each other another time to talk more? I'm due for an appointment, but thanks for the great update!"

I walked away asking the Holy Spirit to resolve this. I knew without prayer and Jesus' involvement that He would not get the glory. I knew that walking 150 feet for the first time in two years was the miraculous work of a loving God. But Barbara herself answered that therapist's questions. In the following weeks, Barbara began going around the facility ministering the love of Jesus to staff and patients alike. There was no question in the patient's eyes who and what had healed her. From that day on, Barbara could be seen often chatting with patients giving them hope and encouragement with the Word of God and talking to them about placing their confidence in Jesus.

In the months to follow, Barbara soared in her personal care, needing only one aide to help her. She loved her supervised treks around the facility with her walker. During our sessions, she would smile gratefully up at me as she easily opened her right hand, freed from the former vise-grip. The Hoyer Lift was never again mentioned. Most notable about the whole thing was that Barbara had now regained peace of mind. She spoke kindly and with clarity to patients, staff and her family.

In a follow-up meeting with her daughter Angela, she shared, "It's really quite an amazing change in mom. We're starting to take her home again for visits. Johnny's taking her to his place next week. We never thought we'd be doing this again."

One year later, at the age of 86, she died peacefully sitting quietly in a comfortable chair having sown seeds of faith and deliverance to patients and staff alike. The Lord set her free and when her purposes were fulfilled on earth, He took her home to be with Him.

REFLECTIONS:

When I cried out in a prayer of desperation to see breakthrough for the seeming hopeless cases, the Lord Jesus revealed a prayerful mental imaging process. He showed me how to teach patients to engage their sanctified imagination with an expectation that Jesus was present to heal them. He assured me that through this process, the Father, through the power of the Holy Spirit, would heal, restore, and build their faith. This experience would then cause His beloved people to draw closer to God, to trust Him, bringing glory to Him. In this case, God brought peace to Barbara's mind and emotions as well as healing to her body.

I was cautioned by the Lord that this process needed to have Him in the middle of it. People at times want to find some answer, some way they can manifest full healing in the world without surrendering to God.

The desire for personal power and control may cause us to want to be able to heal ourselves and others. God surely uses medicine, doctors, surgeries, natural remedies and many avenues to bless His creation, but deep and permanent physical transformation often involves some level of surrender into intimacy with a holy and loving God. He loves to bless His children with healing but His deepest desire is to have close relationship with us.

In this story, Barbara had built a relationship with God in her early years by studying His promises from the scriptures. When the promises of God were again spoken to her, it was like cleansing waters being poured over her soul and mind, refreshing and restoring her. By speaking the truth that "He never leaves us, nor forsakes us," that she is "His beloved and He is hers," she reentered into her early relationship of intimacy with the Lord. This brought the reality of the hope, truth and power of the Word of God that allowed her to regain wholeness in and through Him

God desires that we know Him as Father, as our Creator in whom we can abide. Experiencing Him in us and us in Him brings rest and peace that is beyond anything of this world. This life is a journey of receiving the revelation of our need for God, our need for Yeshua HaMashiach, Jesus Christ. It is a process of coming to recognize our weak ability to manage our lives separate from God's loving presence and guidance. God can, by an act of His love, nurture us in His heart, giving us the completion of our soul's greatest longing to live in His peace and protection regardless of our circumstances. In intimate relationship with Him, God can give us His view of our lives. Drawing close to God, we can enjoy the bliss of sustaining His everlasting presence and peace overall.

SCRIPTURES:

Philippians 4:6-7 Be anxious for nothing, but in everything by prayer and supplication, with thanksgiving, let your requests be made known to God;

and the peace of God, which passes all understanding, will guard your hearts and minds through Christ Jesus. NKJV

Deuteronomy 31:8 "And the Lord He is the One who goes before you. He will be with you, He will not leave you nor forsake you; do not fear or be dismayed." NKJV

Song of Solomon 6:3 "I am my beloved's, and my beloved is mine. NKJV

Jeremiah 31:3 The LORD has appeared of old to me, saying, "Yes, I have loved you with an everlasting love; Therefore with loving kindness I have drawn you." NKJV

15

COCAINE CHAOS TO TRANQUILITY

A human torpedo blasted from the bedroom. Young Tabitha ran straight at me, took a sharp left and rocketed into the kitchen. Her short braids bobbed across her tiny shoulders as she careened past me.

"Sorry, it's been one of those days," Grandma Mildred said as she extended her hand in welcome. A long gray hair escaped her tidy bun and hung loosely down her cheek. Her eyes followed Tabitha's warpath. I watched silent and stunned as the child raced from one end of the room to the other, running circles around every obstacle in her way. She remained in this flight pattern of flurry as Mildred hung up my jacket.

Mildred invited me to sit with her on their cushy floral couch. I was grateful for comfortable seating because I sensed it might take some time to share her story. Mildred choked out difficult memories.

Shaking her head in dazed recollection, she muttered, "My granddaughter Lilly was pregnant with Tabitha, using all kinds of drugs, wild parties, cocaine, even meth. After Tabitha's birth, Lilly's lifestyle got even worse. Nearly drove me crazy thinking about Tabitha right there in the middle of that mess. Druggies coming and going. On Tabbie's third birthday, we begged Lilly to let us help raise her but she wouldn't have it. Poor baby, she's been through a lot in her short five years…."

"Oh my, what did you do?" I said, suppressing a growing knot in the pit of my stomach hearing this tragic story. Mildred rubbed the back of her neck and continued,

"It took a year, but by the grace of God, the courts finally gave her to us."

As I went to my car to gather test equipment, my mind whirled. *Pregnant using heavy drugs….no wonder.* I recalled the studies I had read. *Babies can over-react to movement and touch – even sounds – always on alert. Everything feels threatening to them.* I groaned loudly as I reached for my supplies knowing how difficult these poor children's lives were and I frankly feared for this family's long term challenges.

I rolled the large therapy ball into the living room. As I tipped my burlap bag filled with musical toys -- a small drum, cymbals, jingle bells and a xylophone tumbled onto the floor. Tabitha backed up and darted to her bedroom. Mildred wiped her furrowed brow.

"She runs from everything and everybody. Then I end up doing it on my own," she shared solemnly.

Even with my own limited faith in this moment, I knew Mildred needed a partner she could rely on. This had been a long, lonely journey.

"This has been so hard on you, Mildred. I'm so sorry. I promise you, I'm in this for the long haul. We'll figure this out together."

She looked up at me sheepishly with a hopeful smile. Seeing my sincerity, she responded, "Thanks, I appreciate that."

"We need to test her touch responses." Handing her a stack of cloths ranging from silky satin to rough corduroy, I said, "Rubbing these different textures on her arms should give us some important clues. If it's okay with you, I think the three of us should play together. She'll probably be more comfortable with someone she already trusts."

Mildred rolled her eyes and said, "Don't know about that. She knows we love her, but she screams and runs from us too!"

"Like when?"

"Changing her clothes, getting her into the booster seat, bathing is awful. With just about everything, even playing with toys."

I was beginning to see that Mildred needed more basic understanding to offset fears and frustrations, so I took a breath and dove right in.

"Are you aware that children who are exposed to drugs in utero often are hypersensitive and tend to overreact to normal sensations, like touch and movement, even sounds? I suspect that's what you're up against."

A loud sigh escaped her pursed lips, "Well, that answers a lot." She paused and looked out the window. I could almost see her mind whirling trying to put the pieces together. I was praying I had not overwhelmed her with too much, too soon. I waited, a bit nervous about how she might react. This dear woman had already been through so much.

Then she surprised me. Another part of her seemed to rise up within her. A strong solid woman turned back to me. Looking squarely into my eyes, she asked, "What do we need to do?" Maybe it was her long journey that had trained her to never give up, maybe it was her amazing character, maybe she felt more assured by my offer to partner with her, but in this moment, she was a rock.

Her steadfastness almost bowled me over. Now it was my turn to pause and gather my wits. *Was I ready for this?* My confidence wavered, but then I remembered that God would help us if I trusted Him.

"Well, Mildred we need to establish a baseline so we need to gather some information through some testing. I've got to see what she can tolerate and what's too much for her."

"Okay, let's do it," Mildred said resolutely. She reached out to offer a covenant handshake. As we shook hands, we smiled and she called Tabitha to join us in the living room.

"Listen to this Tabitha!" I said rattling a noisy toy. Grandma and I took turns shaking bells and tapping drums.

"Do you want a turn?" I said, offering the bells to Tabitha. Circling us, she abruptly bolted out of the room, hands over her ears.

Mildred coaxed Tabitha to join us again with a cup of her favorite pudding. She devoured it while she watched Mildred and me roll a large therapy ball between us. As she licked the bowl, I sat on the ball and bounced playfully, holding her doll in my lap.

"Look Tabitha, your dolly likes to take a ride with me," I said. Tabitha smiled cautiously. "You could bounce on the ball with grandma. Would you like to take a turn with her?"

Tabitha agreed so Mildred carefully scooped her up. She sat on the ball and bounced Tabitha briefly, but she wiggled out of Mildred's arms and ran to her bedroom screaming.

"See what I mean?" Mildred said.

"I do see, but it will get better." I touched her shoulder sympathetically. "Let's give her a chance to settle down and try again next week."

Arriving the following week, I set up the stacking blocks, my large peg board, wooden shape puzzle, and laid out coloring books on the kitchen table. Tabitha raced in circles stopping briefly to look. I timed her attention -- 5 to 20 seconds at most.

"Here Tabitha, sit on my lap. Let's have some fun together." Scooping her up I swung her in a wide gentle circle. I felt her little body tense. Mildred watched as I explained I was testing her reaction to movement.

"She hates the park – swings, the slide, teeter-totter – forget it. We just gave up."

"I believe that's the over-sensitivity to movement we talked about," I explained.

"Makes sense," she responded.

I sat holding Tabitha, helping her stack two blocks. Abruptly she jerked her hand from mine. I quickly slid the pegboard in front of us. She wrestled two pegs into the board before wrenching her way out of my arms.

I discussed my observations with Mildred while we watched Tabitha run circles around the table.

"See how as she runs, she tenaciously watches everything as she moves. She's trying to protect herself from anything unexpected. Children who have suffered from heavy drug exposure are often vigilant in a world they perceive as unsafe and overwhelming."

We gazed solemnly. Tabitha's inner struggle was hard to watch.

Forcing a smile, I put my hand on Mildred's sinking shoulder, "We'll get through this together." I finished the testing and packed my bag for the day.

Later that evening, I sat at my desk scoring her tests - a full 20 months behind in motor skills. Reviewing the speech therapist's tests, they showed language at 18 words – no sentences yet.

"Quite delayed in every area for five," I concluded aloud.

I tilted back in my swivel chair and thought -- *Attention span -- five to twenty seconds, tops. Serious over-sensitivity --vigilant -- distractible.* I solemnly closed her file and bowed my head. "Oh Father, show me how to pray. What is your will, your way?"

At the following visit, I explained to Mildred, "We need to make sure she's receiving stimulation that helps her to calm down and focus.

Let's hook up a small swing on the porch and I'll leave the big ball. Gradually, she may become comfortable with it."

"Anything, I'll try anything," responded Mildred.

"Let me teach you how to give her a special massage to help normalize her touch responses." In her bedroom Tabitha leaned back into the cushy beanbag chair, clutching a firm pillow to her chest. Tenderly but firmly, I massaged her arms and legs with a vanilla fragranced oil specially chosen for its calming effect.

"Usually rubbing with firm rather than light pressure is most relaxing. Notice that I'm using long slow strokes."

"Does that feel good, Tabitha?" Mildred asked. Tabitha squirmed but nodded as she nestled deeper in her cozy cocoon.

"It's really important that you look into her eyes as you're massaging. Singing a favorite song can also help."

Mildred cupped her hand and poured out a small amount of oil. She rubbed Tabitha's arms in firm sweeping strokes. Smiling she sang, "Jesus loves the little children, all the children of the world, red and yellow, black and white, they are precious in His sight, Jesus loves the little children of the world." Listening to Mildred's song, it became clear from whom she was drawing strength. I was encouraged that she might be a fellow prayer warrior.

A month passed. We continued the deep touch with lotion, swinging, bouncing and playing. I was praying asking for the mercy of God and His direction for this little precious one. During these weeks of prayer, I sensed an emerging strategy of the Lord. I felt God was reminding me of the power of agreement in prayer that will break the yoke of bondage of the power of darkness over a life. I was being repeatedly reminded of the promise from the scriptures that when two or more are gathered in the name of Jesus Christ, He will be there also and anything that we ask in agreement in His name, the Father in heaven will do. Being reminded of this so frequently, I felt it was a nudge from the Holy Spirit to invite Mildred to pray with me. I began asking the Lord for His timing and grace to talk to her about this. One day in prayer, I sensed a clear directive from the Lord, "Do not even do treatment with Tabitha before first joining in prayer with Mildred each time you meet." *Wow, okay Lord – then you prepare Mildred's heart to desire this as well,* I prayed back to Him.

The next time we met for a session, Mildred set aside some time to talk to me about Tabitha's progress. "I see a little improvement, but she's still screaming and running to her room a lot," Mildred said as she looked adoringly at her grand-daughter across the room. The weariness in her eyes struck me.

I took a breath and asked, "You know, I've been sensing that we should pray together over Tabitha before each session. What do you think?"

Tears pooled in Mildred's grateful eyes, as renewed hope surfaced. She nodded in agreement. *Oh Lord, you're good,* I honored God silently.

Over the following three weeks we prayed faithfully before each treatment session. And then one particular visit, I emptied out my musical instrument bag as Tabitha bounded into the room in her usual style. Snatching up each music toy, Tabitha checked them out briefly and dashed them to the floor.

With new-found conviction and direction, I reached over and took Mildred's hand. We prayed against spiritual strongholds renouncing and taking authority over distraction and chaos. We asked for the peace of God to rest on Tabitha. Mildred picked up Tabitha from the floor and placed her between us on the couch. Closing our eyes, we paused. A profound peace and calm fell and no one moved for several minutes. When we opened our eyes, Tabitha was visibly quiet from head to toe. Her shoulders had stopped their usual bobbing, her normal twisting side to side ceased and her legs weren't swinging. All squirming and fidgeting had virtually stopped.

Tabitha turned her head slowly toward Mildred, lingering there in a deep gaze. She wrapped her arms around Mildred for a long hug and then slid onto the carpet below. As she sat beneath us, we watched in astonishment, as she tapped the drum over and over completely enraptured and delighted. She pounded the drum, changing rhythms and tempos for several minutes. We stared in disbelief. I kept my eye on my watch. Five, six, seven full minutes passed. Mildred and I were speechless. We smiled down at this child whom we barely recognized. We watched in silence except for an occasional, "Wow!" or "Can you believe this?"

Then she further shocked us by reaching for one of the toy cymbals. Turning it over and over, she rubbed its shiny brass surface. Then grabbing its mate, she clanged the two cymbals together until they resounded into a rich crescendo. After several more blissful minutes, I leaned down and offered her the xylophone wand. To our delight, she banged out an original tune for yet another few minutes.

Though we were listening to a primitive little child's song, Mildred and I sat back in stunned joy, appreciating it no less than a Bach concerto. Within that room, between drum beats, cymbals and new songs, the heartbeat of God sounded forth resurrection life.

After that breakthrough day and over the ensuing two months, everything became easier for Tabitha. It was a dramatic turning point. Of course, we continued to follow the directive of the Lord by joining in prayer before every session. I recall a particular day when we were seeing the fruit of God's touch.

"Thanks Tabitha." I said as she handed me a stack of wooden puzzles. She scrambled onto the chair next to me at the table.

"Elephant... monkey," she shouted enthusiastically as she pushed the pieces into the thick wooden board.

Mildred beamed from across the room. "She's trying to color inside the lines on her pictures too, aren't you honey?"

Tabitha looked up smiling and nodded before returning to her play. She exchanged one board for the next. Pointing, she said, "birdy...fish," as she easily shoved the pieces into place.

"Look what you can do, Tabitha!" I said as I patted her shoulder.

"Do you want to show Miss Anita what you made with your big Lego blocks?" Mildred asked.

Tabitha slid out of her chair emitting an excited squeal as she ran happily to her room. Returning shortly, she pulled a little wagon behind her. Stopping in the middle of the room, she turned toward us. She pointed proudly to a Lego tower with a little Lego man perched on top and said, "Look at my man!"

Mildred and I burst into applause. "You made a very tall tower for your special man, Tabitha!" I exhorted.

"Good job, Tabbie!" Mildred resounded.

Tabitha ran over to the big therapy ball and draped her body across it. Looking to grandma, she asked, "Bounce me, please?"

Mildred popped up and swooped Tabitha, twirled her twice and then landed with her on the ball. A lively game of bouncing and rocking ensued.

Mildred and I chimed in together as we sang, "Jesus loves the little children, all the children of the world, red and yellow, black and white, they are precious in his sight, Jesus loves the little children of the world."

Over the next four months, Tabitha's speech therapist reported that Tabitha was speaking in four to five word sentences. Her 20-month gap in development quickly narrowed across the board. Early memories of

Tabitha faded. The child who wiggled out of our arms and ran screaming to her room was replaced by a child who delighted in learning. Fear and vigilance was replaced with safety and trust. Mildred enrolled Tabitha in a class for mildly delayed children who were eventually integrated into normal classrooms. What seemed impossible was not too much for God when the two of us came together in agreement in prayer by a prompting from the Lord Jesus and the Holy Spirit. To Him be all the glory and honor.

REFLECTIONS:

In this experience of breakthrough for little Tabitha, we see a perfect example of God's love and His promise to set the captives free. He loosed the chains of bondage and freed Tabitha to be restored to fullness. This seemed like an impossible situation without a miraculous intervention of a loving God. But our God brings beauty for ashes and He brings dancing for mourning. Mildred was clearly weary under the heavy yoke of this burden she carried for her granddaughter. God moved in response to her fervent prayers and faithful efforts to see Tabitha set free.

God wants to lift the heavy yoke of mental, physical and emotional limitation in all of us. He shows us that if we will yoke with Him and let Him direct us, He will lead us into His rest and peace. The areas in our lives that render us helpless and lost are potential doorways into God's love. He knocks at the door of our hearts, waiting for us to open to His love. He waits for the slightest whisper of His name. In your need, whisper the name of "Jesus" or His Hebrew name, "Yeshua." Call out to Him for help. He is there listening, ready to respond with incomprehensible compassion. Look to Him for your answer. Look to Him for your comfort. Look to Him for your healing.

We can certainly see our prayers answered when we pray alone; however, there are times when we need to pray and agree with one another.

As the Lord guided me in this experience with this family, the strategy from heaven was to pray in agreement with this family member. This is a powerful and amazing promise. Those who grab hold of this truth and apply it will see the move of the Lord. We are encouraged to join together and agree in prayer knowing that God is faithful to His promises.

SCRIPTURES:

Matthew 11:29-30 "Take my yoke upon you and learn from Me, for I am gentle and lowly in heart, and you will find rest for your souls. For My yoke is easy and My burden is light." NKJV

Matthew 18: 19-21 "Again I say to you that if two of you agree on earth concerning anything that they ask, it will be done for them by My Father in heaven. For where two or three are gathered together in My name, I am there in the midst of them." NKJV

Isaiah 61:3 To console those who mourn in Zion, To give them beauty for ashes, the oil of joy for mourning, NKJV

16

BACKBONE OF A MARRIAGE

Beatrice was aging but still beautiful. She was 74, but you would never guess it. As I entered her bedroom, I was struck once again by her stunning sparkling dark eyes high-lighted by a playful pink and green scarf that framed her face. Her full figure was elegantly wrapped in a satin floral robe as she reclined in her daughter's king-size bed, abundant pillows round about her. Beatrice was staying with her daughter Shelly, as Beatrice recovered from gout.

Her lounging robe was partially captured within the crumpled sheets and blankets draped across her bed. An assortment of books, notepads, pens, tissues and a plate of half-eaten fruit lay amid her organized clutter. Today, however, I noticed a Bible in a prominent place, in open view. She saw me take note and slapped her hand heavily on its thick leather cover.

Leaning forward from her backrest, she said, "Yes Anita, I have been praying. I've been praying for Shelly." I could hear the shuffling of clogs across the tile kitchen floor in the distance. It was noon. I imagined that Shelly was preparing lunch for her mom, as she was faithful to do.

"Oh Anita, I just can't take it anymore. Those surgeries just haven't helped her back. She wakes up in pain and goes to bed with it. Lately she's in tears half the time."

Lowering her voice and leaning in closer, she confided, "I know her marriage with Bill doesn't help. The way he treats her…." She paused, lips pursed, but silent. Then she continued, "But she won't leave him." She looked down. A long sigh escaped, "Oh Jesus, Jesus…."

"God is faithful. In the midst of it all, He's faithful," I said trying to reassure her. "I just want the Lord to touch her. I know He can. He did with me," she continued.

She paused. Not waiting for a response, she said, "Would you please talk to her before you leave?"

As Beatrice lamented, my mind drifted to sad images over the months I'd known this family. Shelly's hobbling, bent gait and her anguished, pained face were registering strong in my mind's eye. I recalled Shelly clutching her aching side as she would limp across the kitchen. Then I flashed on her groaning as she rose from her favorite overstuffed chair. Her high tech back brace seemed useless. Surgeons had pinned and fused her herniated discs, but she had gotten little relief.

Beatrice gripped my arm, jolting me back into the moment. "Can we pray?" she pleaded. I bowed my head and joined her passionate petition to God to bring healing and comfort to her daughter. It was a prayer of desperation from a faithful warrior mom.

After finishing Beatrice's therapy session, I promised that I would check in with Shelly before leaving. Walking down the long hallway toward the kitchen, I reflected on how Shelly's brace strapped to her back seemed to mirror the protective armoring I had sensed around her heart. It functioned as a barrier to keep people at a distance.

Will she even trust the most tender approach? I wondered to myself. Or will she rebuff any attempt to be reached? Her nagging pain had become so familiar to her. I wondered if she had given up on God ever healing her. As I approached her, I prayed that the Lord would increase her faith and expectation.

I gave her a quick friendly hug and grabbed a dish towel. Taking the dripping plate she handed off to me, we chatted. A few minutes in, I cautiously probed a bit deeper. "So what have you been up to? You and Bill doing anything fun lately?"

With that, she stopped, looked down into the sudsy water, before angrily slamming the dishrag into the tub. Then she turned abruptly and nearly fled out of the kitchen.

I held my breath and silently prayed, *"Oh dear God, intervene now!"* To my surprise, she slowed her pace, stopped and looked over her shoulder at me. Shaking her head, she grabbed the back of a nearby kitchen chair, swung it around and slumped into it. With no apparent ability to hold back the pent up tidal wave, her shoulders rocked and heaved as tears gushed. Between sobs, she choked out story after story of hateful marital arguments. "Bill hates me. He screams at me the most vicious things. Then I end up screaming back. I can't give him sex - it just hurts my back too much. He says he's disgusted with me. I think - I really think he wants to leave me. God help me," she wailed in despair.

I cautiously placed my arm around her shoulder. As she leaned into the embrace, I deepened the hug and prayed aloud, "Oh God, please bring your compassionate comfort. Bring your peace that passes all understanding in Jesus' Name." I rocked her and hummed a soothing hymn. She relaxed into the rhythmic motion, apparently comforted by the song of God. She released a sigh with a slight shudder. Her breathing slowed. Calmer now, she looked up at me and forced a grateful smile.

"Can I pray more for you, hon?"

"Yes." she agreed, apparently encouraged by the beginning relief she was feeling.

We moved to the living room couch. "Why don't you just sit here?" I said as I prepared a space by fluffing some pillows.

I began by praying for the healing of her back. I reminded aloud that Jesus being crucified on the cross and then being resurrected had already paid this price for her healing. As we prayed, I gently placed my hand on her back over the area of the fused herniated discs. My hand grew warm which is a manifestation of God's love and powerful presence. Startled at first, she said, "Oh, my back is feeling really hot!"

"Yes, I feel the warmth on my hand as well. What you're feeling is God's healing touch of love."

She took a deep breath and I watched her body relax. I sensed God also wanted to touch her wounded heart, the place in her that no longer trusted there was a God who cared for her. The years of verbal and emotional abuse had taken a toll on her sense of worthiness and value. The Lord prompted me to share a bit of my story to encourage her and prepare her to receive more from God.

"Shelly, for a long time I couldn't see myself as precious and valuable, the way God saw me. God started showing me how beautiful I was and how much He loved me despite my failures and mistakes. I had received abuse and critical words also at the hands of wounded people. I needed to find out what God says about me. Over time, I learned to start believing the truth about who I really am. Sometimes, I thought too little of myself, feeling self-hatred. Yet, at other times, I felt defensive about the truth of my shortcomings, not being able to take healthy correction so I could grow in honesty about myself. Gradually, as God showed me how He saw me, I began to see myself as precious and loveable. Eventually, I began to evolve into that healed strong person that God said that I was. Then I could see my mistakes and forgive myself and out of that merciful view of myself, I could make needed changes. I also started to have more mercy for others. Shelly, I had to forgive myself and others for the many mistakes, the wrongs that were done against me. God showed me that we are all hurting people who need God's grace, kindness and love. It really stunned me when God showed me how much He loved the people who had hurt me." I paused as she sat quietly registering my words.

"Shelly, do you want to pray about this as well?"

"Oh, yes," she said. She seemed more receptive and hopeful.

I prayed now with gentleness but authority, "Lord Jesus, we break the power of harmful words that have been spoken over Shelly, that have wounded Shelly's soul. In your precious name, Jesus, we take authority over accusing spirits that have tormented her mind, will and emotions. We ask you Lord to break the power of depression, hopelessness and fear. We know Lord that you do not bring a spirit of fear, but of love, power and a sound mind. We ask you Lord Jesus to heal her today in your mighty name. And Lord Jesus, just as you did for me and so many others, would you now show Shelly how you see her?" Her shoulders relaxed and her eyelids closed in grateful relief and rest.

As she sat quietly, waiting in God's presence, I also asked, "And Lord Jesus, would you also reveal to Shelly what happened to Bill in his life that caused him to treat Shelly the way he has?"

I encouraged Shelly to ask the Lord, herself, saying, "Just ask God, Shelly – what happened to Bill that caused him to treat me the way he did?"

She whispered the question to Him and then she waited expectantly. A minute passed and then suddenly her eyes popped open wide and she blurted out, "I just saw my husband as a little boy. His dad was hitting him. He was screaming horrible things at Bill!" Shelly was visibly shaken but I encouraged her to ask, "Show me more, Lord."

She closed her eyes, again pondering this picture further, repeating, "Yes, show me more about this." Compassionate tears welled up and rolled down her cheeks. "He's so little. I see him lying in a corner all curled up crying. He was so scared. I never saw how his father's rage affected him."

From this place of compassion, Shelly sincerely prayed a spontaneous prayer for her husband. "Oh God – heal his heart from those awful words. I think I need to forgive Bill too…Oh God, please forgive me for the things I've said and done that hurt him, too." Silence – a minute passed. "But – wait - now I see Jesus weeping." Silence again. "Oh my. Jesus is weeping and looking at me and Bill. He's reaching out His arms to both of us." Silence ensued and then she said, "Jesus is so sad -- for my pain too! Oh, I can feel how much He loves me!" I watched as she silently reveled in God's affection for her. Her face beamed, reflecting the adoring gaze she was receiving from God.

After several minutes, she said, "It's strange. Now I'm seeing myself at five years old, all dressed up like a princess. I'm wearing mama's high heeled shoes. I have a toy tiara on my head. I used to love to dress up when I was little." She paused to take it all in.

"Ask Him to reveal to you why He's showing you this. What does it mean?" I suggested. "Go ahead and ask Him, Shelly," I encouraged.

"Why are you showing me this, God?" she asked. A minute or two passed while we waited. Then in a near inaudible whisper, she shared, "O-o-oh, God is showing me, this is how He sees me -- as His princess. I can hardly believe it." A single tear rolled down her cheek as she gazed on this amazing picture and personal revelation.

I smiled. My eyes grew moist as I thanked God for His faithfulness and kindness toward this dear daughter. Under the weighty reality of God's love for her, she was able to let God exchange lies for His truth that healed her heart.

"That's right, Shelly," I said in a soothing tone. "Just relax and receive the fullness of this understanding. Let His love heal your heart."

I waited for a few more minutes while she reclined on the couch and silently rested in God's loving presence. Glancing at my watch, I said gently, "Shelly, it's time for me to go, but I can let myself out. I encourage you to just rest and receive more from Him."

I leaned down and kissed her atop her head like a Papa might show affection to one of His favorite kids. "Just rest here on the couch for a while in His presence and let Him minister the fullness of what He wants to give you today." I paused at the door before quietly closing it behind me. I was enjoying seeing her in this restful repose with a peaceful glow on her face. I sensed God was doing a deep lasting work in her. I walked out thanking God, wondering what all He had done.

After that session, it was determined by the medical team that Beatrice no longer required homebound services so I discharged her from my caseload. Seven months passed before I had an occasion to be back in touch with the family. At that point, I received a voicemail from Shelly regarding her needing help ordering supplies for Beatrice, so I returned her call. After completing the business at hand, I asked,

"So how are you doing? How's your back?"

"Oh, so much better!" She then relayed a wonderful story.

"I didn't have a chance to tell you that day we were together," she continued, "but the week before your visit, I was in so much pain that the hospital x-rayed my back again. On the images, they saw a surgical pin that broke off and was floating around my spine. So they scheduled surgery to remove the pin. The surgery was scheduled two days after your visit."

"Really? Oh goodness." My heart was pounding.

"Well, even though I was feeling so much better after our prayers, I went in. And of course, they x-rayed again to determine the exact location of the pin before doing surgery. Well, it's funny, Anita. They came out and said they were going to have to take more pictures 'cause they couldn't find it! They x-rayed me three more times! I saw a lot of white coats come and go that day. I was there a long time. Finally the doctor said, 'well, we don't see it and without knowing the exact position, we just have to cancel the surgery for now!' The metal piece never showed up again. It vanished or dissolved or something!"

I was stunned. I had heard stories from others of how after prayer, metal pins and hardware sometimes dissolved or vanished. This was the first time I had seen Jesus touch one of my patients in that way. We laughed together in joyful celebration and praised God! "So how are you feeling lately?" I queried.

"I'm taking long walks again and sleeping real good! You know my back pain used to be like a seven or eight on a scale of one to ten before we prayed. Now it's usually a two or three at most!"

"That's great!" I exclaimed.

"My back's just getting better and better. Some days I barely notice any pain at all! I haven't felt this good in years! Bill and I are doing much better too! I told him what God showed me that day. I think it really touched him. He's treating me a lot better. He's taking me to Florida next month for my birthday. We both love the beach! Anytime I start to get mad at him, I just see him as that little boy in the corner and my heart melts all over."

"Well I couldn't be happier for you Shelly. That's great news!"

"Thanks for taking the time with me that day, Anita."

"You know it was really your mom's love and faithful prayers for you!"

"I know! She's so relieved and happy for me! Oh, yeah, Bill wants to take her on our next road trip after Florida. I think he finally appreciates her -- and me for that matter!"

REFLECTIONS:

Shelly needed to experience the manifest presence of a God who loves her. Her marital strife had left deep heart wounds which caused her to be vulnerable to receive negativity and darkness that cloaked Shelly's mind and emotions. Accusations and abuse had rendered her hopeless and despondent, further blocking her ability to believe in and receive the reality of God's love for her. Abuse often builds distrust and creates resistance to the truth that there is a merciful kind Father God who actually desires to touch, heal and restore.

Shelly needed an encounter with the God of Love who could show her the truth of who she is to Him and how much He loves her. Challenged by life's fierce trials, Shelly was brought to her knees before a loving God. There in her brokenness, she was tenderly and dramatically encouraged and restored. Shelly and I renounced the powers of darkness who were trying to deceive and discourage her, trying to rob her of the blessing and joy that the Lord had for her. She turned to God's Spirit of love and kindness and she was changed, body, soul and spirit.

God also gave Shelly compassion for her husband by letting her see him through God's eyes of love and grace. This prompted Shelly to experience compassion toward her husband so reconciliation could begin. As with Shelly, God can, and is eager to do the same for you. He loves us all the same. Though we've made mistakes and suffered trials, God just wants us to turn to Him and ask "Who do you say that I am?" "How do you see my circumstances, the people around me, my past, my future?" so we can walk in the truth and abundance of His love and acceptance. When we experience the profound love of a God of mercy and grace, we can be transformed by this astounding love.

SCRIPTURES:

Hebrews 4:15 For we do not have a High Priest who cannot sympathize with our weakness, but was in all points tempted as we are, yet without sin. NKJV

Matthew 14:14 And when Jesus went out He saw a great multitude; and He was moved with compassion for them, and healed their sick. NKJV

Isaiah 61:1 The Spirit of the Lord is upon me, because the Lord has anointed me to preach good tidings to the poor; He has sent me to heal the broken-hearted, to proclaim liberty to the captives and the opening of the prison to those who are bound; KJV

John 1:5 And the light shines in the darkness, and the darkness did not comprehend it. NKJV

John 8:32 And you shall know the truth, and the truth shall make you free. NKJV

2 Timothy 1:7 For God has not given us a spirit of fear, but of power and of love and of a sound mind. NKJV

17

WALKING IN JOY AND PEACE

I was thrown off guard, but I steadied my voice and continued the phone conversation. "Well Kevin, it seems that Dr. Perkins and your physical therapist, Mary, are just concerned. They want to be sure that you're completely safe there in your home, since your back surgery and.... "

"I really don't need any more help," he interrupted, nearly yelling now. "My physical therapist is QUITE ENOUGH. I like my house the way it is. THANKS ANYWAY."

Kevin was definitely rushing me off the phone. For an initial occupational therapy call arranging a routine visit, I was clearly not getting a standard response. Knowing how crucial this visit was, I pressed in, saying,

"Well, Kevin, I appreciate your concerns. It sounds like you don't want anyone disrupting how you do things. I can assure you that I'll be very respectful. I would only be coming to help."

I was trying to waylay Kevin's concerns, trying everything I knew to build rapport and trust.

"I LIKE things the way they are. Got EVERYTHING I need," he insisted again.

"Well, Kevin maybe you can help me out here. You see, I have this doctor's order that requires I do a home safety assessment so that your physical therapist is allowed to keep coming. So maybe we can just have this one visit. Then maybe you can help me figure out if there's any more I could do for you. How does that sound?"

Silence. I sensed that he was processing my carefully worded statement implying he may need to cooperate in order to continue his homebound physical therapy.

In that moment, I prayed that his heart would be encouraged and softened. From what the physical therapist had told me, Kevin was definitely at risk for falls. She was frankly scared for her patient.

"Well, just this ONCE, but you'll see EVERYTHING'S fine here," he repeated.

Maybe it's the extreme pain he's in, I thought as I hung up the phone.

Reports I'd read showed that Kevin was suffering with debilitating back and leg pain since his laminectomy, which involved removal of a portion of vertebrae, as well as fusion of a third of his spine. I knew he was trying to go easy on the pain meds, so he didn't build a dependency.

I had to have two more phone conversations over the next week in order to build a modicum of trust with Kevin, enough for him to set a day and time to meet. Driving through torrential Texas rains that day, I prayed for wisdom and grace to build rapport with Kevin. I was bracing myself and asking God to prepare Kevin's heart and mind to receive whatever God had for him. I pulled up to his modest 1960s home. Turning off my Toyota, I tilted my seat back to reflect for a moment before going in.

In prayer, I asked the Holy Spirit to fill Kevin's home with God's presence. I asked the Lord to show me ways to support his heart and to guide me and give me words to help him. Right there, resting in my car, I sensed God's still small voice giving me a simple question to ask Kevin, 'When in your life were you the most joyful and peaceful?'

I strained to understand more clearly. I heard again in my spirit, "Ask him, 'when in your life were you the most joyful and peaceful?'" Knowing nothing about this patient's past, I found this a provocative question. I had learned not to paraphrase but to try to follow the specific words of the Lord. I grabbed my notepad and wrote the question exactly as I'd heard it, word for word. I reread it, several times, committing it to memory, 'when in your life were you the most joyful and peaceful?'

Kevin swung the door open. Barely saying hello, he turned and hobbled in front of me leaning heavily on his cane, gripping his hip for support. His late-forties pudgy body wavered unsteadily as we neared the hallway. He slid his free hand along the wall for extra support as he trekked ahead of me. Determined, he curtly said,

"As you can see, I'm fine here," narrowly missing a waste basket in his path. He led me rapidly through his small home, careening through an obstacle course of clothes piled high and stacks of books. Avoiding eye contact with me, he pressed ahead, only occasionally stopping to look at me to drive home the point,

"As I said on the phone, I clearly don't need anybody else in here. I got everything I need." I made mental notes of potential safety hazards, gingerly pointing out to him cluttered traffic ways, but Kevin quickly rebuffed each comment as 'nothing to worry about.'

At one point, rounding a corner into a hallway, I gently asked, "So how is your pain level right now, Kevin? On a scale from one to ten, ten being unbearable."

Leaning on his cane, a wince torqued his face as he stroked his balding head. His brow wrinkled. He looked at me and through a breathy whisper, he said, "Oh probably an eight or nine." I caught a wisp of moisture in his eyes, but he jerked his gaze from me quickly and darted ahead on his journey, muttering, "I'll be okay, I'll be okay...."

Heading toward the couch, he haltingly rounded a coffee table, grazing his leg. Fortunately, I was able to catch his arm, recovering him from a near fall. It was apparent Kevin was not safe in his home. As he eased himself down into the pillowed corner of his sofa, he let out a deep groan of pain.

"Oh, Kevin how frequently is it like this?"

"Pretty much every day. Sometimes it's a six or seven, but mostly like this. I don't like the pain drugs. Take 'em sometimes. They make me groggy."

"I see. Must be getting exhausting to deal with all that pain, though. Sorry, Kevin," I sincerely offered. My heart went out to the man.

He paused. "Yeah, thought it'd be better by now. Going on 16 weeks," he pondered, looking out the window. I wondered to myself how often had he stared out of that window, questioning when, if ever, he'd venture out on his own again. Looking back to me, he noticed my sympathetic gaze. With that, he cleared his throat, straightened his shoulders and the mask went up again. With a slight quake in his voice, he asserted, "Just need to be left alone. That's all I need."

My mind raced, trying to sense from the Lord how I was going to convince him that he needed me to return. I prayed in quiet desperation for God's way through this. Frankly, it seemed impossible.

We sat across from each other on the couch and just as I was thinking I had lost the battle, I looked at a far wall. I smiled. There hung a huge colorful rendering of the face of Jesus. The artist had captured the light of Christ's radiant countenance.

"My! What an amazing painting of Jesus!" I exclaimed. "The Lord's beauty through that piece is truly breathtaking."

Kevin looked over at it and for the first time, I saw him soften, as he smiled a gentle smile, "Yeah, yeah, I know," he said, "that's probably why I'm still able to move at all. I told the surgeon that someone or something was moving his hands during that surgery."

This was the opening that was needed. I launched out with a fresh boldness.

"Isn't it wonderful how Jesus brings such comfort and healing for today," I offered with genuine enthusiasm. My caution and trepidation were replaced with zeal.

"I know, I know. If you only knew where I've been. But a lot has happened," he shared solemnly. "Sometimes I don't know what to make of anything, anymore."

The Holy Spirit brought to mind the question that He had given me to ask Kevin. I knew time was short and it needed to be asked. When God gives me an assignment, I feel compelled to be faithful and do what I'm directed to do.

I explained to Kevin that as a strong believer in Jesus, sometimes when I pray for people, God gives me specific words to speak.

Though Kevin looked at me blankly, I pursued.

"On my way over I was praying for you and I sensed that I was to ask you a very specific question, Kevin."

With an expression which was a cross between cynicism and mild curiosity, he said, "Really, what is it?"

Looking deeply into his eyes, confident not in myself, but in the Lord, I firmly but kindly said, "The question is 'when in your life were you the most joyful and peaceful?'"

He looked fully stunned. He stared at me, speechless. Seconds passed. His face slowly transformed from stun to clear excitement as he shared,

"You know, it is so amazing. Really that you should ask me that. It was just 2 days ago, yeah, Tuesday night on the phone…." he continued.

"Really, what do you mean?"

"I was having a long talk with an old friend. I actually used those exact words. I said to her in our conversation, 'you know the time in my life I was the most joyful and peaceful was when I was in a Christian community.' Because you see I've recently been exploring Buddhism, but also wondering about my connection to Jesus and the church."

I was struck by God's perfect order and timing of giving me that question to ask him. Kevin shook his head in astonishment.

"Wow, that had to be from God. You don't even know me or what I've been through," he said shaking His head. "That's amazing."

At this point, the barricades came down. Kevin shared his deep heart with me for a full half hour. He gave details of a rich deep walk he'd enjoyed with the Lord Jesus for 15 years of his life, woven into a Christian community. He explained that he'd been anointed and trained in the gifts of the Holy Spirit, gifts of healing, words of knowledge and ministry of deliverance. With excitement, he shared how he'd seen dozens of people healed and delivered from bondages and set completely free.

"But it got messy. I got into a couple of ugly arguments with leaders and walked away from the whole thing. I had a real lucrative business and started traveling. Collecting antique cars. Had an airplane and a couple of yachts. Then my wife and I started arguing and she left me. I just got sicker and sicker and then this back thing. Lost everything. Mostly from the medical bills. In the past year, I've been looking into Buddhism but I just don't know."

"That is quite a journey, Kevin. It sounds like you're at a crossroads," I offered.

"Guess you could say that," he reflected. "Buddhism teaches compassion, it's true, but what I've seen is that only the name of Jesus

Christ has the power to heal and deliver people from their deep suffering. That's been striking me as true compassion."

He brought the conversation back to how amazed he was that I was given that specific question to ask him. He saw it as a supernatural gift to him from God.

"You know, only God can know our private thoughts and considerations. It's this thought that's been making me wonder about returning to Jesus and a community of believers, but I don't know."

At this point, he requested prayer. As we prayed, the peace and presence of God was so strong that Kevin ended the night saying he saw our meeting as a divine appointment to help him to return to his first love, Jesus Christ – the One who brought joy and peace. Not the peace that the world gives through creature comforts but the peace of mind and spirit that personal relationship with Jesus offers. Needless to say after that conversation, I was welcomed back to provide treatment on a regular basis.

Over the following four weeks, we worked on safety issues in the home, clearing walking pathways to avoid possible falls. Teaching a man with rough edges who is rather set in his ways was tricky, though.

"Don't you girls have anything better to do than to move my things around? My books and piles of clothes are just where I like 'em," Kevin complained.

Sometimes, I'd return the following week to have to clear pathways all over again. Teaching him how to pace himself to conserve energy to lower his risk for falls was also met with resistance.

"Awww, I been doin' it this way for years. Now you want me to take deep breaths and stop and waste my time on these silly exercises?" Gratitude and appreciation were not his forte, but occasionally I could see some small indications of a softening of his heart.

"I'm reading the Bible again and comparing it to my Buddhist literature. Do you know Buddha himself said that he was not a god and if he followed any deity, it would have been Jesus?"

I could see his tendency toward negativity beginning to melt in the face of my sincere concern for him. It was also apparent he was receiving the authentic love of the Father and Jesus in our prayer times together. He seemed more joyful after prayer. His pain levels were lowering and he seemed more hopeful about his future.

On the fifth week, however I arrived at Kevin's home and found him in extreme pain. He answered the door, rocking and weaving, leaning precariously over his cane, while he clutched his left hip. Between moans and pants, he explained that earlier in the day, he had fallen asleep in front of his computer. Apparently, as he dozed, his positioning pillows slipped down causing his head, neck and back to lurch forward in an awkward position. He awoke with overwhelming pain and muscle spasms in his buttocks, back and hips.

He shared that the physical therapist had just left a half hour before I arrived.

"I felt better for a while, but it's all back," he continued. "I think...I think maybe I should go to the emergency room."

Knowing Kevin, I knew it had to be bad if he was considering the emergency room.

"Sure Kevin. We should have it looked at," I agreed.

"But first, first...would you...would you be willing to pray with me? It always helps when we pray."

"Of course," I said. I thought it might calm him for the ambulance ride to the hospital.

We walked slowly to the bedroom. With my arm encircling his back, I eased him down on the bed. Slowly, choking back tears, he agonizingly leaned back. He squirmed, groaning loudly trying to find a tolerable position. With great reluctance, he took several minutes to position himself and gradually released his grip on his hip.

"Maybe we should go right now, Kevin," I cautioned.

"No, no. Please. Let's do this," he insisted.

Slowly, in cautious increments, he raised his hands into the air, assuming a semblance of a posture of worship. I led us into worshipping God, proclaiming His goodness for all He was about to do, as we often agreed in our prayer time together. However, this time it seemed the spiritual atmosphere was electric.

Kevin released a long low "o-o-oh," as I saw his body sink more comfortably into the bed. I was grateful to see this. As Kevin lifted his arms higher in fervent prayer, I perceived the Lord's anointing presence pour into the room.

I finally relaxed myself. A few minutes passed. As I prayed, I was reminded of a specific word God had given me for Kevin earlier in the day. I knew it was time to speak it.

"Kevin, I sense the Lord saying, if in a flock of 100 sheep, only one is lost, the Lord who is his shepherd will seek out the one lost sheep to bring it home."

As I completed the word, Kevin burst into tears.

Through sobs, he explained that he was crying with joy because just moments before I spoke this, the Lord had been giving him a vision of Jesus going out seeking and finding the one lost sheep. Kevin knew it was the Lord saying that He was seeking and rescuing Kevin. My word was confirming the Lord's message to him that God was drawing Kevin back into the sheepfold.

As I prayed, the Lord was directing me to lay my hands on Kevin's body in different areas, his back, shoulders, hips and legs and over his heart. Kevin suddenly gasped saying,

"Oh, do you know that wherever you are laying your hands, I feel heat over that area. Oh, I feel such peace. Thank you, Jesus."

I also felt guided to share a loving corrective word to Kevin during this prayer ministry. The word to Kevin was "hush your lips from grumbling and complaining. Use your tongue only for praising God." Again, Kevin was deeply moved.

"That's amazing. Just yesterday, I heard Joyce Meyers on TV. And I was totally convicted that it was a message for me about the way I speak. She was talking about people guarding their tongues against grumbling and complaining. The Lord is confirming that word right now. Wow!"

I could see that in this prayer time, the anointing of the glory of the Lord was powerfully present to help Kevin transform his habit of complaining. It was apparent that God was bringing all the help Kevin needed for this change, just as Kevin's heart was ripe for conviction with a willingness to transform his words from negativity to gratitude and honoring.

Spontaneously, Kevin exuberantly exploded in praise to God, as never before, "You are a wonderful amazing beautiful God. Your love endures forever. You are our healer. Blessed be the Lord of Hosts. You are faithful. Hosanna in the highest. You never leave us nor forsake us." As Kevin's soul was willing, the Lord began renewing Kevin's mind in the moment. It was truly a gift to watch the Lord touch Kevin's mind, soul and spirit.

Twenty to twenty-five minutes passed as we just praised and worshipped, while we asked the Lord Jesus to complete the healing He'd begun, giving God all the glory.

Then the most extraordinary thing happened! Kevin sputtered out, "You're, you're not going to believe this. I barely can believe it myself and I'm the one feeling it."

"What is it?" I probed.

A minute passed. I remained silent, sensing something unusual was taking place. Finally he said, "For the first time, the first time since, since the surgery, I feel nothing!"

"What do you mean?" I asked.

"No pain, whatsoever!" he said. Another long pause followed. I sat speechless.

"It's gone, completely gone!" he exclaimed.

At this point, Kevin began to raise himself cautiously from the bed. I reached out to help him. Waving me away, he said, "No, I'm okay. I'm really okay," he said in a tone of stunned amazement.

"Oh, Kevin I don't think you should move on your own." I still had not adjusted from the picture of his extreme pain and distress of a half hour earlier.

Paying no attention to me, he pulled himself into sitting. To my amazement, he was visibly moving faster. He swung his legs over the edge of the bed and pushed up into standing easily. He grabbed his cane but I noticed that though he held it in his hand, he really wasn't using it as he walked toward me. He then made his way through the bedroom door and turned to go down the hallway.

Everything was happening way too fast for me. It was so surreal.

A wide grin covered over his beaming face, as he suddenly turned back toward me, saying,

"Wait, wait, watch this!" He extended his cane toward me to hold.

I hesitantly took it saying, "Are, are you sure?" I stammered. Ignoring my well intentioned caution, he pronounced confidently,

"Watch this!" With long even strides, he walked briskly toward me saying,

"Really, I have no pain!" Then he exclaimed with glee, "We don't need those big arenas where people get out of their wheelchairs and walk! We got it going on right here at my house!"

That's the Glory of God. Praise Jesus.

With some waxing and waning in his healing process over the next few months, Kevin never again returned to his early level of pain and instability, always steadily improving. Now he is a sign and wonder to so many, proclaiming that Jesus and the Holy Spirit were sent to bring the lost sheep back home, to set the captives free from pain and misery. Kevin talks about a return to church community life. He feels drawn back into business as well, saying,

"To make another million, but this time," he said, "I'll give it away, to people who need it. I don't need much. I've got the Lord Jesus!"

REFLECTIONS:

Kevin was at a crossroads in his spiritual life. In the midst of it, a fervently loving God wooed him back through a most incredible process. Isn't it amazing that God gives us free will to choose Him? Not manipulating or cajoling with demands or rules, but through a love that honors intelligent reason and compassionate consideration. Then just at the right moment, through a sovereign touch of healing and deep impartation of wisdom into Kevin's spirit, God drew him back to Himself offering him healing and a renewed life in Christ.

Many times during my sessions with Kevin, I had to pray and receive wisdom and understanding from heaven to hear specific things to ask of or share with Kevin. Clearly, only God could have known what Kevin needed. Regularly, I leaned heavily on God through prayer, completely dependent on Him to know how to help Kevin. I had learned to follow Jesus' model when He said that He could do nothing of Himself, but only what He saw the Father in heaven doing.

The Holy Spirit was drawing Kevin back to a time of greatest joy and peace in his life, which was a period of personal relationship with his Lord Jesus Christ. Often, people think they have a problem with Christ, but they more often have trouble with religious self-righteous people. Even Jesus had a problem with the religious Pharisees calling them white-washed tombs filled with dead men's bones. A loving relationship with Yeshua or Jesus Christ is what will bring joy and peace to any of us.

SCRIPTURES:

John 5:19 Then Jesus answered and said to them, 'Most assuredly, I say to you, the Son can do nothing of Himself, but what He sees the Father do; for whatever He does, the Son also does in like manner. NKJV

John 14:10 …The words I speak to you I do not speak on My own authority; but the Father who dwells in Me does the works. NKJV

Matthew 18: 11-13 For the Son of Man has come to save that which is lost. What do you think? If a man has a hundred sheep, and one of them goes astray, does he not leave the ninety-nine and go to the mountains to seek the one that is straying? And if he should find it, assuredly, I say to you, he rejoices more over that sheep than over the ninety-nine that did not go astray. NKJV

Proverbs 21:23 Whoever guards his mouth and tongue keeps his soul from troubles. NKJV

Nehemiah 8:10 Do not sorrow, for the joy of the LORD is your strength. NKJV

Philippians 4:7....and the peace of God, which surpasses all understanding, will guard your hearts and minds through Christ Jesus. NKJV

CONCLUSION

My hope is that these stories have inspired you to see more clearly that there is a God of love and compassion in your midst. I realize that praying for people in your walk of life can feel daunting; however the God of goodness wants to partner with you. Through it, you will see Him move and more importantly, draw you into more intimate relationship with Him. He is faithful to meet you right where you are.

I am just an ordinary person. I am a person with flaws and weaknesses like anyone else. I am a work in progress. We all are. These stories have little to do with me and everything to do with the love, compassion and power of God. Place yourself in the stories and you will see that you can be that ordinary person watching breakthrough for yourself, family, friends, co-workers, patients, or customers because He is the same God; He never changes. He will do the same for you. He is the one with the love, compassion and capacity to move, to touch, to restore. He is the God of goodness.

I was a young therapist when it all began. I had a few skills and I knew I could help some people; but I also saw that many conditions and needs were far beyond what I could bring. I was clear that I was little and limited. Fortunately, God quickly showed that He is big and bountiful in His love and desire to bless. That's simply all I could trust. As a matter of fact, it was apparent that the weaker and less capable I felt, the more He seemed able to move mightily.

I needed to not allow my limited thinking to get in the way of His big heart. Knowing I had NOTHING, He could be SOMETHING BIG for someone in need. His mercy and kindness is extraordinary. Over many months, He graciously taught me expectancy – to expect and see – what He could and wanted to do. He is love. He doesn't know how else to be.

I saw over time that He is a faithful God who is ALWAYS looking for a way that He can bless, restore and redeem. So if after praying, I didn't see an instant obvious shift, I had to look for what He was doing, possibly in the person's heart to draw them to Him. It is my experience that when you pray there is always movement in the spirit, even if you don't see it in the natural. I began to see a consistent phenomenon, which was an astounding shift in the person's countenance. The person will often speak of a profound sense of well-being, joy and peace after prayer. Further, people often exude a glow about them; they speak of a deep abiding peace that they had never felt before. It occurs so frequently that I have come to call it the Signature of God.

When there are delays in seeing the fullness of healing, the challenge is to not become discouraged. Prayers cause transformation and shifts at different levels for different purposes. Do not lose heart. There is great value in the process of deepening prayer while you wait for the fullness of your healing for yourself or others.

In quiet time with the Father, Jesus and the Holy Spirit, profound transformation is often experienced. If the focus of the prayer is on deepening relationship with God, it will always bear fruit of intimacy bringing deeper peace, joy and love to your soul and spirit. As you continue to seek Him, you will feel and experience the washing of His loving touch over you. He will transform places of your heart that need more of Him and need a deeper understanding of how much you are loved and treasured by Him.

After time spent with God, you will feel the refreshing of your soul. Your mind, will and emotions will be cleansed of the impact of the stress of circumstances and pressures of life. God will show you that He is there, caring for you, guiding you, restoring and encouraging you. In His presence, He will relieve emotional as well as physical pain, refreshing you while you wait on and believe for the fullness of your healing.

Each time you come before Him in worship and prayer, come with expectancy for Him to move in the midst of your encounter. I encourage people to come with expectancy (to expect and see). Never give up. Trust Him. He is a faithful loving Father. He will bring His transforming peace and joy in your journey of intimacy with Him.

In closing, I invite you to receive this word into your spirit from our God of love:

I love you with an Everlasting Love –
   It never wanes; I never grow tired of blessing.

My Love always waits patiently for you
   to turn even slightly toward Me with a willing heart,
to hear from Me, to be touched.
I weep when my sweet child remembers
   to look to Me in the midst of her trouble, confusion.
If you only believed this were true,
   you would encounter Me, at every turn.

Unbelief is so rampant in the world.

   And the enemy of your soul so quick

to feed a thought

that I am not with you or don't care about you.

The real battle in this life

   Is to remember who you are

in Me and through Me.

Oh, if you prayed to see into the spiritual reality

   and saw My true grief when you try to go it alone,

even for a moment.

   That was never how I planned it.

I created you as My beloved,

   to walk with Me, in joy, passion and fulfillment,

   not tomorrow, not some day –

but in this moment,

   and the next…

and the next…

     and forever…

It is waiting for you,

But you must let Me in.

I stand and wait with bated breath,

   that you would turn from your distraction,

your self-concern, survival thoughts and plans –

I wait as with the anticipation of an eager lover,

that you would but give Me a glance, a smile,

a hopeful thought about Me, to let Me in –

so I can help, relieve, direct,

but mostly just to hold, caress,

   to rock, calm, and bring peaceful reassurance,

like any true lover –

   who would say –

"I'm here, I'll help and everything's going to be fine –

     you're not alone, I'll walk through this with you."

ABOUT THE AUTHOR

Anita Andreas has enjoyed thirty years in private medical practice as an occupational therapist weaving medicine with her walk of faith in Yeshua HaMashiach, Jesus Christ. Drawing from expertise in pediatrics, psychiatric and physical disabilities, she holistically treats children, adults and the elderly. Anita inspires faith for a move of God in medical, educational and spiritual spheres. She considers her greatest blessing to be her four wonderful sons, their lovely wives and families, her deepest delight, her six beloved grandchildren.

WWW.ANITAANDREAS.COM

www.ingramcontent.com/pod-product-compliance
Lightning Source LLC
Chambersburg PA
CBHW031957040426
42448CB00006B/394